Victor W. Watton,
Robert M. Stone & Rebecca Watton

Religion and Society

Teacher's Resource Pack

THIRD EDITION

HODDER
EDUCATION
AN HACHETTE UK COMPANY

The Publishers would like to thank the following for permission to reproduce copyright material:

Photo credits p.108 © Getty Images/Matt Cardy; **p 111** *top* © foodfolio/Alamy, *middle top* © OlgaLIS – Fotolia.com, *middle bottom* © Douglas Freer – Fotolia.com, *bottom* © Steve Stock/Alamy.

Acknowledgements

Every effort has been made to trace all copyright holders, but if any have been inadvertently overlooked the Publishers will be pleased to make the necessary arrangements at the first opportunity.

Although every effort has been made to ensure that website addresses are correct at time of going to press, Hodder Education cannot be held responsible for the content of any website mentioned in this book. It is sometimes possible to find a relocated web page by typing in the address of the home page for a website in the URL window of your browser.

Hachette UK's policy is to use papers that are natural, renewable and recyclable products and made from wood grown in sustainable forests. The logging and manufacturing processes are expected to conform to the environmental regulations of the country of origin.

Orders: please contact Bookpoint Ltd, 130 Milton Park, Abingdon, Oxon OX14 4SB. Telephone: (44) 01235 827720. Fax: (44) 01235 400454. Lines are open 9.00–5.00, Monday to Saturday, with a 24-hour message answering service. Visit our website at www.hoddereducation.co.uk

Cover photos : *l* © Mark Edwards/Still pictures; *m* © Kipa/Corbis; *r* © Neil Higginson/Rex Features.
Illustrations by Barking Dog.
Typeset in 10.5 and 12pt Arial by Fakenham Photosetting Limited, Fakenham, Norfolk.
Printed in Great Britain by Hobbs The Printers, Totton, Hants.

A catalogue record for this title is available from the British Library

ISBN: 978 0340 975527
Religion and Society Pupil's Book, Third Edition: 978 0340 975510
Religion and Society Pupil's Book, Foundation Edition, Third Edition: 978 0340 975640
Religion and Society Revision Guide, Third Edition: 978 0340 975657

CONTENTS

INTRODUCTION

This teacher guide is intended to provide a full teaching scheme for Unit 8 'Religion and Society based on a study of Christianity and at least one other religion' of the Edexcel GCSE Religious Studies specification. It supports the third edition of the main or foundation *Religion and Society* student's book.

How the guide is organised

Each section within the guide is dedicated to one of the sections of the specification and the student's book. Each topic within the section is then divided into lessons – comprising a lesson plan followed by any additional student resources needed for that lesson such as Starter Sheets and Fact Sheets.

Each lesson plan includes:

- the objectives of the lesson
- the learning outcomes of the lesson
- prior learning for the lesson
- a list of resources needed for the lesson
- a starter activity with suggested timing
- a main activity with suggested timing
- a plenary activity with suggested timing
- suggestions for extension
- suggestions for reinforcement
- suggestions for ICT
- suggestions for homework
- suggestions for assessment.

At the end of each section is an end of section test allowing students to complete an exam-focused summative assessment.

Appendices at the back include:

- a generic lesson plan and worksheets for each section (ideal for when you need cover)

- the Edexcel generic mark scheme
- mark schemes for the end of section tests
- target setting advice for the end of section tests and for the examination
- links showing coverage of the Citizenship Programme of Study
- links showing coverage of the PSHE Programme of Study
- extra resources covering how the economy functions, including the role of business and financial services.
- All of the resources are on the accompanying CD-ROM in Word® format, allowing you to adapt the lessons and resources to your individual needs. In light of recent initiatives, the lesson outcomes may need editing to, 'all students will...', 'most students will...' or 'some students will'.

Planning the course

The lesson plans have been written so that the Unit can be delivered in 65 lessons. Although they appear in section order, all of the sections are free standing so that they can be taught in any order (although this would involve some changes to the prior learning and target setting elements).

About the authors

Victor Watton and Bob Stone have been Senior Examiners for GCSE Religious Studies for many years and the materials indicate the levels of response expected. Rebecca Watton is a practising RS teacher with a special interest in ICT and RS.

LESSON 1: INTRODUCTION TO STUDYING UNIT 8

Lesson objectives • To investigate the reasons for studying GCSE Religious Studies. • To outline the course content and its timings. • To gain agreement on the need for serious study and keeping to deadlines.	**Lesson outcomes** By the end of the lesson students should be able to: • explain why they are following a GCSE course in Religious Studies • outline what they will study in the course, and when they will study each topic • agree to study the course seriously and keep to deadlines.
Prior learning Key Stage 3 Religious Studies	**Resources** • Starter Sheet 1 • Fact Sheet 1 • Fact Sheet 2 • Fact Sheet 3A (for short course over two years) • Fact Sheet 3B (for full course Years 9–11 with Unit 8 exam in Year 10) • Fact Sheet 3C (for full course Years 9–11 with Unit 8 exam in Year 11) • Fact Sheet 3D (for the first part of a full course with two lessons a week)

10 mins	**Starter activity** 1. Put Starter Sheet 1 on students' desks before they come in. 2. As students come into the room, ask them to put as many reasons as they can think of into each column.
35 mins	**Main activity** 1. Use Fact Sheet 1 (Why take GCSE Religious Studies?) to explain why the students are sitting in the RS lesson, allowing opportunities for comment and discussion from the students. The read-through and explanation should be used to dispel misconceptions and to engender enthusiasm for the course. 2. Hand out copies of Fact Sheets 2 (Specification outline) and 3 (Scheme of Work for Unit 8) and go over them with the class, emphasising any points you wish (for example, the timing of tests and examinations). 3. Make sure that all of the students understand the need for hard work, keeping to deadlines and respect for others' opinions in discussion lessons.
5 mins	**Plenary activity** 1. Ask the students to re-visit their Starter Sheet and change any points in light of what they have learned. 2. Set the homework.

Extension Extra homework – find out what the Catechism of the Catholic Church is.	**Reinforcement** Make sure less able students do the starter activity in pairs with a more able partner so they have help in writing down their ideas.
Homework Ask the students to ask two or three adults why they would or would not use the Bible to guide them in making moral decisions.	**Assessment** Observation of student participation and responses.
	ICT • The starter activity could be done on an interactive whiteboard. • The various fact sheets could be displayed on an interactive whiteboard.

STARTER SHEET 1

Reasons for taking GCSE Religious Studies	Reasons for NOT taking GCSE Religious Studies

? ?

FACT SHEET 1

Why take GCSE Religious Studies?

- It is an interesting course in which you look at the influence of Christianity and one other religion on topics such as:
  - making moral decisions
  - human rights in the UK
  - genetic engineering
  - environmental issues
  - infertility treatments
  - transplant surgery
  - war and peace
  - bullying
  - capital punishment
  - attitudes to drugs
  - attitudes to alcohol.

- Many employers (especially the police, armed forces and caring professions) regard GCSE Religious Studies as a good qualification. It involves a lot of thinking skills and writing skills, and shows that you are aware of other people's beliefs and the nature of the society you live in.

- It helps you to think through some of the big issues of life that adults contemplate all the time.

- It helps to remove the ignorance that causes prejudice, hatred and violence (many wars are caused through misunderstandings about religion).

- Religious Studies protects you from indoctrination (being made to accept a set of beliefs without questioning them). It gives you the opportunity to explore religious and moral beliefs in a safe and questioning environment so that you can become sure of your own beliefs and explain them clearly to others.

- It is another GCSE qualification for you!

RELIGIOUS STUDIES IS NOT ABOUT MAKING YOU 'RELIGIOUS', IT IS ABOUT ENABLING YOU TO THINK FOR YOURSELF ABOUT RELIGIOUS AND MORAL ISSUES WHICH EVERYONE FACES IN ADULT LIFE.

? ?

? ?

FACT SHEET 2

Specification outline

You will be following the Edexcel GCSE course in Religious Studies, Unit 8. If you are taking the short course GCSE, you will take the examination at the end of Year 11. If you are taking the full course, you will study two units and will either take one examination at the end of Year 10 and the other at the end of Year 11, or will take both examinations in Year 11. If you gain a grade G or above in either the full or short course, you will receive a GCSE certificate from Edexcel.

Unit 8: Religion and Society based on a study of Christianity and at least one other religion

Section 1 – Religion: Rights and responsibilities
- How Christians make moral decisions
- Human rights
- Why it is important to take part in democratic and electoral processes
- Christianity and genetic engineering

Section 2 – Religion: Environmental and medical issues
- Environmental issues (global warming, pollution, resources)
- Christianity and the environment
- One non-Christian religion and the environment
- Medical treatments for infertility
- Different attitudes to infertility treatments in Christianity and one other religion
- Different attitudes to transplant surgery in Christianity and one other religion

Section 3 – Religion: Peace and conflict
- The United Nations and world peace
- Why wars occur
- Attitudes to war in Christianity and one other religion
- Attitudes to bullying in Christianity and one other religion
- Religious conflicts within families
- Attitudes to forgiveness in Christianity and one other religion

Section 4 – Religion: Crime and punishment
- The need for law and justice
- Why justice is important in Christianity and one other religion
- The issue of capital punishment
- Attitudes to capital punishment in Christianity and one other religion
- Legal, social and health problems caused by drugs and alcohol
- Attitudes to drugs and alcohol in Christianity and one other religion

? ?

? ?

FACT SHEET 3A

Scheme of Work for Unit 8 Short Course

Term 1	Term 4
Introduction Rights and responsibilities (topics 1–9)	Peace and conflict (topics 6–11) Crime and punishment (topics 1–4)
Term 2	**Term 5**
Rights and responsibilities (topics 10–11) Environmental and medical issues (topics 1–6)	Crime and punishment (topics 5–11) Revision
Term 3	**Term 6**
Environmental and medical issues (topics 7–11) Peace and conflict (topics 1–5)	Revision and exam

Assessment dates

Section 1 test _____

Section 2 test _____

Section 3 test _____

Section 4 test _____

Year 10 exam _____

Mock exam _____

Course requirements

All students will be expected to:
• attend regularly
• take part sensibly in class discussions
• be punctual to lessons
• complete homework
• listen to and respect class teachers and other students
• revise for tests and exams.

I understand that I am working towards a GCSE in Religious Studies and agree to the course requirements.

Name of student _____

Signature _____

Parent/guardian signature _____

? ?

? ?

FACT SHEET 3B

Scheme of Work for Unit 8 as first part of full course

Y9 Term 1	Y10 Term 1
Introduction Rights and responsibilities (topics 1–9)	Peace and conflict (topics 10–11) Crime and punishment (topics 1–8)
Y9 Term 2	**Y10 Term 2**
Rights and responsibilities (topics 10–11) Environmental and medical issues (topics 1–8)	Crime and punishment (topics 9–11) First section of other unit
Y9 Term 3	**Y10 Term 3**
Environmental and medical issues (topics 9–11) Peace and conflict (topics 1–9)	Revision and exam for Unit 8 Finish Section 1 of other unit and begin Section 2

Assessment dates

Section 1 test _____   Section 4 test _____

Section 2 test _____   Year 10 exam _____

Section 3 test _____   Mock exam _____

Course requirements

All students will be expected to:
- attend regularly
- take part sensibly in class discussions
- be punctual to lessons
- complete homework
- listen to and respect class teachers and other students
- revise for tests and exams.

I understand that I am working towards a GCSE in Religious Studies and agree to the course requirements.

Name of student _____

Signature _____

Parent/guardian signature _____

? ?

? ?

FACT SHEET 3C

Scheme of Work for Unit 8 as second part of full course

Y10 Term 2	Y11 Term 2
Rights and responsibilities (topics 1–9)	Crime and punishment (topics 1–11)
Y10 Term 3	**Y11 Term 3**
Rights and responsibilities (topics 10–11) Environmental and medical issues (topics 1–9)	Revision and exam
Y11 Term 1	
Environmental and medical issues (topics 10–11) Peace and conflict (topics 1–11)	

Assessment dates

Section 1 test _____

Section 2 test _____

Section 3 test _____

Section 4 test _____

Year 10 exam _____

Mock exam _____

Course requirements

All students will be expected to:
- attend regularly
- take part sensibly in class discussions
- be punctual to lessons
- complete homework
- listen to and respect class teachers and other students
- revise for tests and exams.

I understand that I am working towards a GCSE in Religious Studies and agree to the course requirements.

Name of student _____

Signature _____

Parent/guardian signature _____

? ?

? ?

FACT SHEET 3D

Scheme of Work for Unit 8 as the first part of a full course with two lessons a week

Y10 Term 1	Y10 Term 3
Introduction Rights and responsibilities (topics 1–11) Environmental and medical issues (topics 1–11)	Revision Examination First section of other unit
Y10 Term 2	
Peace and conflict (topics 1–11) Crime and punishment (topics 1–11)	

Assessment dates

Section 1 test _____   Section 4 test _____

Section 2 test _____   Year 10 exam _____

Section 3 test _____   Mock exam _____

Course requirements

All students will be expected to:
- attend regularly
- take part sensibly in class discussions
- be punctual to lessons
- complete homework
- listen to and respect class teachers and other students
- revise for tests and exams.

I understand that I am working towards a GCSE in Religious Studies and agree to the course requirements.

Name of student _____

Signature _____

Parent/guardian signature _____

? ?

LESSON 2: TOPIC 1.1 THE BIBLE AS A BASIS FOR MAKING MORAL DECISIONS

Lesson objectives	**Lesson outcomes**
• To investigate the use of the Bible in making moral decisions. • To explore why some Christians use only the Bible to make moral decisions.	By the end of the lesson students should be able to: • explain why some Christians use only the Bible to make moral decisions • explain their own opinion about using the Bible for moral decision making • explain why some people may disagree with them.

Prior learning	**Resources**
Lesson 1: Introduction to studying Unit 8	• Student's Book pages 1–3 • Starter Sheet 2

10 mins	**Starter activity** 1. Put Starter Sheet 2 on students' desks. Students should be encouraged to start the task as soon as they sit down. 2. Follow this up by reading page 1 of the Student's Book with the whole class so that they understand what they will be studying in this section.
30 mins	**Main activity** 1. Choose students to come to the front of the class and use their Starter Sheets to complete a table on the board. 2. Read through pages 2 and 3 of the Student's Book, encouraging the students to amend/add to the list of reasons on the board for using the Bible as a basis for making moral decisions. 3. Discuss the reasons against using the Bible as a basis for making moral decisions, amending the list on the board where necessary. 4. Make sure that everyone has a copy of the completed list.
5 mins	**Plenary activity** Read the exam focus advice on page 3 of the Student's Book, then set the homework question.

Extension	**Reinforcement**
Set question **d** from page 3 of the Student's Book, either as an extra class activity or as an extra homework: 'The Bible is the best guide we can have when making moral decisions.' i Do you agree? Give reasons for your opinion. ii Give reasons why some people may disagree with you. At least one of the points of view should be Christian with reasons from that religion.	Less able students should be paired with a more able partner for the starter activity and should be informed that they only need to give one reason for their homework.

Homework	**Assessment**
Set question **c** from page 3 of the Student's Book: Explain why some Christians use only the Bible when making moral decisions.	Answers to the homework question marked according to the Edexcel mark scheme (Appendix 5).
	ICT The results of the discussions and the plenary activity could be done on an interactive whiteboard.

STARTER SHEET 2

Put two or three reasons in each column.

Reasons why the Bible might give good guidance in making moral decisions	Reasons why the Bible might NOT give good guidance in making moral decisions

LESSON 3: TOPIC 1.2 THE AUTHORITY OF THE CHURCH AS A BASIS FOR MAKING MORAL DECISIONS

Lesson objectives	**Lesson outcomes**
• To investigate the authority of the Church for Christians. • To explore why some Christians use only the Church's teachings for making moral decisions.	By the end of the lesson students should be able to: • explain why some Christians use only the Church's teachings for making moral decisions • explain their own opinion about the authority of the Church • explain why some people may disagree with them.
Prior learning Topic 1.1 The Bible as a basis for making moral decisions	**Resources** • Student's Book pages 4–5 • Key Words Sheet 1.1 • Video clip of the Pope (for example, from www.uspapalvisit.org)

10 mins	**Starter activity** Give the students Key Words Sheet 1.1. Ask them to draw a picture or write a word in the prompt column to help them to remember each word.
30 mins	**Main activity** 1. Show a video clip of the Pope and then discuss why Catholics may follow the guidance of the Pope. 2. Divide the students into pairs and ask them to use pages 4 and 5 of the Student's Book to answer question **c** from page 5: 'Explain why the Church has authority for Christians when making moral decisions.'
5 mins	**Plenary activity** 1. Explain the exam focus advice on page 11. 2. Apply the mark scheme below to the question 'Do you think Christians should use only the teachings of the Church for making moral decisions?' to explain the difference between a brief reason and a developed reason in this type of question. Also explain that these questions are meant to be quite easy. It is expected that a candidate who will end up with a grade D will get full marks for these questions.

for a personal response with: • one brief reason (for example, the Church knows what is right)	1 mark
for a personal response with: • two brief reasons • or one developed reason (for example, the Church knows what is right, because people like the Pope and bishops have more contact with God)	2 marks

Extension Students could find out more information about the Magisterium of the Catholic Church.	**Reinforcement** Less able students should be paired with a more able partner for the starter activity and the second part of the main activity.
Homework Set question **b** from page 5 of the Student's Book: Do you think Christians should use only the teachings of the Church for making moral decisions? Give two reasons for your point of view.	**Assessment** Answers to the main activity and the homework questions marked according to the Edexcel mark scheme (Appendix 5).
	ICT The video could be displayed using an interactive whiteboard or a projector.

KEY WORDS SHEET 1.1

Key Word	Meaning	Your Prompt
Bible	the holy book of Christians	
Church	the community of Christians (with a small c it means a Christian place of worship)	
conscience	an inner feeling of the rightness or wrongness of an action	
Decalogue	the Ten Commandments	
democratic processes	the ways in which all citizens can take part in government (usually through elections)	
electoral processes	the ways in which voting is organised	
Golden Rule	the teaching of Jesus that you should treat others as you would like them to treat you	
human rights	the rights and freedoms to which everyone is entitled	
political party	a group which tries to be elected into power on its policies (for example, Labour, Conservative)	
pressure group	a group formed to influence government policy on a particular issue	
situation ethics	the idea that Christians should base moral decisions on what is the most loving thing to do	
social change	the way in which society has changed and is changing (and also the possibilities for future change)	

Religion and Society Teacher's Resource Pack Third Edition © Hodder Education, 2009

LESSON 4: TOPIC 1.3 THE ROLE OF CONSCIENCE AS A GUIDE IN MAKING MORAL DECISIONS

Lesson objectives	Lesson outcomes
• To investigate the role of conscience in making moral decisions. • To explore why some Christians believe conscience is the most important guide in making moral decisions.	By the end of the lesson students should be able to: • explain why some Christians believe conscience is the most important guide in making moral decisions • explain their own opinion about the role of conscience • explain why some people may disagree with them.

Prior learning	Resources
• Topic 1.1 The Bible as a basis for making moral decisions • Topic 1.2 The authority of the Church as a basis for making moral decisions	Student's Book pages 6–7

15 mins	**Starter activity** 1. Display the key word definition of conscience on the board: 'An inner feeling of the rightness or wrongness of an action'. Alongside it put an example such as: 'Feeling guilty when you do something you know is wrong'. 2. Ask students to write down examples of when their conscience has guided them in doing or not doing an action. 3. Select students to put their answers on the board, allowing a small amount of discussion.
25 mins	**Main activity** Read through pages 6–7 of the Student's Book, using discussion to ensure that everyone understands the role of conscience and the arguments among Christians about its authority.
5 mins	**Plenary activity** Read through the exam focus and exam tip (page 7 of the Student's Book) to explain how to answer evaluation questions.

Extension	Reinforcement
Differentiation by outcome should be possible.	Less able students could be advised to give only one reason for part **i** and one reason for part **ii** of the homework.

Homework	Assessment
Set question **d** from page 7 of the Student's Book: 'Your conscience is the best guide for deciding what is right and what is wrong.' **i** Do you agree? Give reasons for your opinion. **ii** Give reasons why some people may disagree with you. At least one of the points of view should be Christian with reasons from that religion.	Answers to the homework question marked according to the Edexcel mark scheme (Appendix 5).
	ICT The starter activity could be done on an interactive whiteboard.

LESSON 5: TOPIC 1.4 SITUATION ETHICS AS A GUIDE FOR MAKING MORAL DECISIONS

Lesson objectives	**Lesson outcomes**
• To investigate situation ethics. • To explore why some Christians use only situation ethics for making moral decisions.	By the end of the lesson students should be able to: • explain why some Christians use only situation ethics for making moral decisions • explain their own opinion about situation ethics • explain why some people may disagree with them.

Prior learning	**Resources**
• Topic 1.1 The Bible as a basis for making moral decisions • Topic 1.2 The authority of the Church as a basis for making moral decisions • Topic 1.3 The role of conscience as a guide in making moral decisions	• Student's Book pages 8–9 • Starter Sheet 3

15 mins	**Starter activity** 1. Give out Starter Sheet 3 for students to complete in pairs. 2. Discuss their answers and then read through the first three paragraphs on page 8 of the Student's Book to lead them to the idea that situations may change people's attitudes to moral rules.
25 mins	**Main activity** 1. In pairs, students should read through the rest of page 8 and page 9 of the Student's Book, making a list of arguments in favour of and against Christians using situation ethics. 2. Check students' answers orally, individually or by displaying a correct list on the board.
5 mins	**Plenary activity** Remind students of the evaluation technique from the exam focus on page 7 of the Student's Book, and tell them there will be a test on the key words for Section 1 in the next lesson.

Extension	**Reinforcement**
Differentiation by outcome should be possible.	Make sure less able students are paired with a more able partner for the starter and main activities.

Homework	**Assessment**
Set question **d** from page 9 of the Student's Book: 'Christians should always do the most loving thing.' **i** Do you agree? Give reasons for your opinion. **ii** Give reasons why some people may disagree with you. At least one of the points of view should be Christian with reasons from that religion.	Answers to the homework question marked according to the Edexcel mark scheme (Appendix 5).
	ICT The starter answers and the correct answers to the main activity could be displayed on an interactive whiteboard.

STARTER SHEET 3

Answer Yes or No to the following questions:

1. Is it always right to tell the truth?

2. Is it always right to return things you have borrowed?

3. Is it always right to obey your parents?

4. Is it always right not to kill people?

LESSON 6: TOPIC 1.5 WHY SOME CHRISTIANS USE A VARIETY OF AUTHORITIES IN MAKING MORAL DECISIONS

Lesson objectives • To investigate the use of a variety of authorities in Christian moral decision making. • To explore why some Christians use a variety of authorities to make moral decisions.	**Lesson outcomes** By the end of lesson 7 students should be able to: • explain why some Christians use a variety of authorities to make moral decisions • explain their own opinion about Christian moral decision making • explain why some people may disagree with them.
Prior learning • Topic 1.1 The Bible as a basis for making moral decisions • Topic 1.2 The authority of the Church as a basis for making moral decisions • Topic 1.3 The role of conscience as a guide in making moral decisions • Topic 1.4 Situation ethics as a guide for making moral decisions	**Resources** • Student's Book pages 2–11 • Key Words Sheet 1.2

10 mins	**Starter activity** 1. Give out Key Words Sheet 1.2 for students to complete individually. 2. Collect them in for marking.
30 mins	**Main activity** Divide the students into groups to prepare presentations on the following topics: • Topic 1: Why some Christians use the Bible, but sometimes have to use other sources of authority (pages 2, 3 and 10 of the Student's Book) • Topic 2: Why some Christians use the Church, but sometimes have to use other sources of authority (pages 4, 5 and 10 of the Student's Book) • Topic 3: Why some Christians use their conscience, but sometimes have to use other sources of authority (pages 6, 7 and 11 of the Student's Book) • Topic 4: Why some Christians use situation ethics, but sometimes have to use other sources of authority (pages 8, 9 and 11 of the Student's Book).
5 mins	**Plenary activity** Make sure that each group knows what they have to do to have their presentations ready for the next lesson.

Extension Students could find out more information for their presentation by researching on the internet, for example: www.cofe.anglican.org, www.catholic-ew.org.uk, www.baptist.org.uk, www.methodist.org.uk.	**Reinforcement** Make sure that the less able students are doing the Topic 1 presentation as this is easier.
Homework Finish presentations for next lesson.	**Assessment** Marking of Key Words Sheet 1.2.
	ICT PowerPoint or other software could be used for the presentations.

KEY WORDS SHEET 1.2

Draw lines to link the key word with its correct meaning.

Key Word	Meaning
Golden Rule	the holy book of Christians
pressure group	the community of Christians (with a small c it means a Christian place of worship)
social change	an inner feeling of the rightness or wrongness of an action
human rights	the Ten Commandments
situation ethics	the ways in which all citizens can take part in government (usually through elections)
political party	the ways in which voting is organised
Bible	the teaching of Jesus that you should treat others as you would like them to treat you
Decalogue	the rights and freedoms to which everyone is entitled
democratic processes	a group which tries to be elected into power on its policies (for example, Labour, Conservative)
Church	a group formed to influence government policy on a particular issue
conscience	the idea that Christians should base moral decisions on what is the most loving thing to do
electoral processes	the way in which society has changed and is changing (and also the possibilities for future change)

LESSON 7: TOPIC 1.5 WHY SOME CHRISTIANS USE A VARIETY OF AUTHORITIES IN MAKING MORAL DECISIONS

Lesson objectives
- To investigate the use of a variety of authorities in Christian moral decision making.
- To explore why some Christians use a variety of authorities to make moral decisions.

Lesson outcomes
By the end of the lesson students should be able to:
- explain why some Christians use a variety of authorities to make moral decisions
- explain their own opinion about Christian moral decision making
- explain why some people may disagree with them.

Prior learning
- Topic 1.1 The Bible as a basis for making moral decisions
- Topic 1.2 The authority of the Church as a basis for making moral decisions
- Topic 1.3 The role of conscience as a guide in making moral decisions
- Topic 1.4 Situation ethics as a guide for making moral decisions

Resources
Student group presentations

5 mins	**Starter activity** Students should set up their presentations.
35 mins	**Main activity** 1. Group presentations from lesson 6 on why some Christians use a variety of authorities to make moral decisions, with those students not presenting taking notes. 2. After each presentation students should be given the opportunity to ask the presenters questions, which may lead to some group discussions.
5 mins	**Plenary activity** Set and discuss the homework question using the exam tip on page 11 of the Student's Book.

Extension
Differentiation by outcome should be possible.

Reinforcement
Less able students could be given photocopies of a more able student's notes on the presentations.

Homework
Set question **d** from page 11 of the Student's Book:
'You need more guidance than the Bible when you have to make a moral decision.'
i   Do you agree? Give reasons for your opinion.
ii Give reasons why some people may disagree with you.
At least one point of view should be Christian with reasons from that religion.

Assessment
Answers to the homework question marked according to the Edexcel mark scheme (Appendix 5).

ICT
PowerPoint or other software could be used for the presentations.

LESSON 8: TOPIC 1.6 HUMAN RIGHTS IN THE UNITED KINGDOM

Lesson objectives • To investigate human rights in the UK. • To explore why human rights laws are important.	**Lesson outcomes** By the end of lesson 9 students should be able to: • explain why it is important for the UK to have human rights laws • explain their own opinion about human rights laws • explain why some people may disagree with them.
Prior learning Key Stage 3 Citizenship lessons on human rights	**Resources** • Student's Book pages 12–13 • Four copies of Homework Sheet 1 for each student

10 mins	**Starter activity** 1. Ask the students to make a list of what human rights they think they have living in the UK. 2. Select some students to write their answers on the board, making a list of human rights.
30 mins	**Main activity** 1. Read through the list of human rights on pages 12–13 of the Student's Book, allowing discussion where necessary. 2. Discuss the *Guardian* report about migrant workers (page 12 of the Student's Book). 3. Amend the list on the board as necessary and ask students to copy it out (or give out copies).
5 mins	**Plenary activity** Explain the questionnaire (Homework Sheet 1) and how it should be given out to one adult aged over 70, one aged between 50 and 69, one aged between 30 and 49 and one aged between 18 and 29. Also explain the importance of the results being ready for the next lesson.

Extension • Differentiation by outcome should be possible. • Students could be asked to work out a results chart that could be used to record the questionnaire findings and present them to the class in the next lesson.	**Reinforcement** If possible pair less able students with stronger partners to do the homework.
Homework Students should ask four adults to complete the questionnaire (Homework Sheet 1).	**Assessment** N/A
	ICT An interactive whiteboard could be used to record the starter activity results and their amendments.

HOMEWORK SHEET 1

Questionnaire on human rights

As part of my GCSE Religious Studies course, I am investigating whether people think human rights laws are important. I would be grateful if you would help me with this by giving brief answers to these questions.

1. What is your age?	2. Do you think it is important to have laws to protect our rights?	3. Give reasons for your answer to question 2.	4. Which of the laws listed below would you like to get rid of? Circle your choices.
			Your human rights are: • the right to life • freedom from torture and degraded treatment • freedom from slavery and forced labour • the right to liberty • the right to a fair trial • the right not to be punished for something that wasn't a crime when you did it • the right to respect for private and family life • freedom of thought, conscience and religion • freedom of expression • freedom of assembly and association • the right to marry or form a civil partnership and start a family • the right not to be discriminated against in respect of these rights and freedoms • the right to own property • the right to an education • the right to participate in free elections

Religion and Society Teacher's Resource Pack Third Edition © Hodder Education, 2009

LESSON 9: TOPIC 1.6 HUMAN RIGHTS IN THE UNITED KINGDOM

Lesson objectives	**Lesson outcomes**
• To investigate human rights in the UK. • To explore why human rights laws are important.	By the end of the lesson students should be able to: • explain why it is important for the UK to have human rights laws • explain their own opinion about human rights laws • explain why some people may disagree with them.
Prior learning Lesson 8	**Resources** • Student's Book pages 12–13 • Completed questionnaires • Starter Sheet 4

15 mins	**Starter activity** Display the results chart for the questionnaire findings (Starter Sheet 4) on the board and ask a range of students to record their questionnaire answers (copies could be printed and given to students).
25 mins	**Main activity** 1. Discuss the questionnaire findings. 2. Ask students to read through pages 12–13 of the Student's Book again, making a list of any rights they think they could do without. 3. Ask students to come up to the board and list any rights they could do without (copies could be printed and given to students). 4. Discuss their answers.
5 mins	**Plenary activity** Set and discuss the homework questions, using the exam tip on page 13 of the Student's Book.

Extension Differentiation by outcome should be possible.	**Reinforcement** • Make sure that less able students are in groups where they will be supported and that they are given copies of the questionnaire findings. • Advise less able students that one reason for their own point of view and one for the opposite will be sufficient for the second homework question.

Homework
Set questions **c** and **d** from page 13 of the Student's Book.
c Explain why it is important for the UK to have human rights laws.
d 'Human Rights laws are only useful for people who break the law.'
  i Do you agree? Give reasons for your opinion.
  ii Give reasons why some people may disagree with you.
	Assessment
	Answers to the homework questions marked according to the Edexcel mark scheme (Appendix 5).

	ICT The starter activity and part 3 of the main activity could be done on an interactive whiteboard.

STARTER SHEET 4

Results chart of the findings on human rights

Q1 Age	Q2 YES	Q2 NO	Q3 Reasons	Q4 Laws that should go
1. (70+)				
2. (50–69)				
3. (30–49)				
4. (18–29)				

Religion and Society Teacher's Resource Pack Third Edition © Hodder Education, 2009

LESSON 10: TOPIC 1.7 WHY HUMAN RIGHTS ARE IMPORTANT FOR CHRISTIANS

Lesson objectives	**Lesson outcomes**
• To investigate human rights in Christianity. • To explore why human rights are important for Christians.	By the end of the lesson students should be able to: • explain why human rights are important for Christians • explain their own opinion about Christian attitudes to human rights • explain why some people may disagree with them.

Prior learning	**Resources**
Topic 1.6 Human rights in the United Kingdom	• Student's Book pages 14–15 • Starter Sheet 5

10 mins	**Starter activity** 1. Put a copy of Starter Sheet 5 on the desks before students arrive. 2. Ask the students to complete the sheet as soon as they sit down. 3. Make a tally chart (on a blank copy of Starter Sheet 5) of students' answers.
30 mins	**Main activity** 1. In pairs, students should read page 14 of the Student's Book and write down four reasons why human rights are important for Christians. 2. Read and discuss why some human rights cause problems for some Christians (page 15 of the Student's Book). 3. Refer back to the student answers from the starter activity, discussing any changes they might now want to make.
5 mins	**Plenary activity** Set the homework and discuss the exam tip on page 15 of the Student's Book.

Extension	**Reinforcement**
• Differentiation by outcome should be possible. • Question **d** on page 15 of the Student's Book could be set as an extra homework.	Less able students should be paired with a more able partner for the starter activity and part 1 of the main activity.

Homework	**Assessment**
Set questions **b** and **c** from page 15 of the Student's Book: **b** Do you think Christians should accept all human rights laws? Give two reasons for your point of view. **c** Explain why human rights laws are important for Christians.	Answers to the homework questions marked according to the Edexcel mark scheme (Appendix 5).
	ICT The starter activity and part 3 of the main activity could be done using an interactive whiteboard.

STARTER SHEET 5

Put a Yes or a No in each column.

Human rights law	Would most Christians think this is a good law?	Might this law cause problems for some Christians?
the right to life		
freedom from torture and degraded treatment		
freedom from slavery and forced labour		
the right to liberty		
the right to a fair trial		
the right not to be punished for something that wasn't a crime when you did it		
the right to respect for private and family life		
freedom of thought, conscience and religion		
freedom of expression		
freedom of assembly and association		
the right to marry or form a civil partnership and start a family		
the right not to be discriminated against in respect of these rights and freedoms		
the right to own property		
the right to an education		
the right to participate in free elections		

LESSON 11: TOPIC 1.8 WHY IT IS IMPORTANT TO TAKE PART IN DEMOCRATIC AND ELECTORAL PROCESSES

Lesson objectives	Lesson outcomes
• To investigate democratic and electoral processes. • To explore why it is important to take part in democratic and electoral processes.	By the end of the lesson students should be able to: • explain why it is important to take part in democratic and electoral processes • explain their own opinion about taking part in democratic and electoral processes • explain why some people may disagree with them.

Prior learning	Resources
• Topic 1.6 Human rights in the United Kingdom • Topic 1.7 Why human rights are important for Christians	• Student's Book pages 16–17 • Video of a parliamentary debate from www.parliamentlive.tv

15 mins	**Starter activity** 1. Show a brief clip from a parliamentary debate (free video coverage of live debates is available from www.parliamentlive.tv, which also has free archive footage). 2. Discuss the students' opinions about the importance and effectiveness of MPs.
25 mins	**Main activity** 1. Read through pages 16–17 of the Student's Book with the class, allowing plenty of reference back to what they said in part 2 of the starter activity. 2. Discuss why some people might not want to take part in democratic and electoral processes.
5 mins	**Plenary activity** 1. Discuss what might happen to the country if only old people bothered to vote. 2. Set the homework and discuss the exam tip on page 17 of the Student's Book.

Extension	Reinforcement
Differentiation by outcome should be possible.	Less able students should be advised that they only need to give one reason for part **i** and one reason for part **ii** of the homework question.

Homework	Assessment

• Set question **d** from page 17 of the Student's Book:
d 'It doesn't matter whether or not you vote.'
  i Do you agree? Give reasons for your opinion.
  ii Give reasons why some people may disagree with you.
• Revise for the key words test next lesson.
	Answers to the homework question marked according to the Edexcel mark scheme (Appendix 5).

	ICT The starter video could be shown via an interactive whiteboard or data projector.

LESSON 12: TOPIC 1.9 CHRISTIAN TEACHINGS ON MORAL DUTIES AND RESPONSIBILITIES

Lesson objectives	Lesson outcomes
• To investigate Christian teachings on moral duties and responsibilities. • To explore why Christian teachings on moral duties and responsibilities are important for Christians.	By the end of the lesson students should be able to: • explain why Christian teachings on moral duties and responsibilities are important for Christians • explain their own opinion about Christian teachings on moral duties and responsibilities • explain why some people may disagree with them.
Prior learning	**Resources**
• Topic 1.1 The Bible as a basis for making moral decisions • Topic 1.2 The authority of the Church as a basis for making moral decisions • Topic 1.3 The role of conscience as a guide in making moral decisions • Topic 1.4 Situation ethics as a guide for making moral decisions • Topic 1.5 Why some Christians use a variety of authorities in making moral decisions • Topic 1.8 Why it is important to take part in democratic and electoral processes	• Student's Book pages 18–19 • Key Words Sheet 1.3

10 mins	**Starter activity** 1. Put Key Words Sheet 1.3 on students' desks to complete as soon as they sit down. 2. Collect it in for marking.
25 mins	**Main activity** Divide the class into three sets of groups to make posters: • Group 1 should answer the question 'Which of the Ten Commandments are important today and which ones are not?' giving reasons for their choices. • Group 2 should answer the questions 'What is meant by "Am I my brother's keeper?"' and 'Why is it important for Christians today?' • Group 3 should answer the questions 'Why is the Parable of the Sheep and the Goats important for Christians?' and 'Should it be important for everyone?'
10 mins	**Plenary activity** Display and discuss the posters. Set the homework question and go over the exam tip on page 19 of the Student's Book.

Extension	Reinforcement
More able students could be asked to apply the Golden Rule to capital punishment.	Less able students should be paired with a more able partner for the main activity.

Homework	Assessment
Set question **c** from page 19 of the Student's Book: Explain why the Parable of the Sheep and the Goats leads some Christians to bring about social change.	• Marking the key words test. • Answers to the homework question marked according to the Edexcel mark scheme (Appendix 5).
	ICT The main activity could be done using presentation software such as PowerPoint rather than making posters.

KEY WORDS SHEET 1.3

Fill in the blanks in the table.

Key Word	Meaning
Bible	
Church	
conscience	
Decalogue	
democratic processes	
electoral processes	
Golden Rule	
human rights	
political party	
pressure group	
situation ethics	
social change	

LESSON 13: TOPIC 1.10 THE NATURE OF GENETIC ENGINEERING, INCLUDING CLONING

Lesson objectives	Lesson outcomes
• To investigate genetic engineering. • To explore why genetic engineering is an important, but controversial, issue.	By the end of lesson 14 students should be able to: • explain why genetic engineering is an important, but controversial, issue • explain their own opinion about genetic engineering • explain why some people may disagree with them.

Prior learning	Resources
• Topic 1.6 Human rights in the United Kingdom • Topic 1.8 Why it is important to take part in democratic and electoral processes	• Student's Book pages 20–21 • Video on the human genome project

10 mins	**Starter activity** 1. Show a brief video on the human genome project. This could be sourced from the internet, for example www.pbs.org/wgbh/nova/genome/program.html. 2. Discuss what they have seen.
30 mins	**Main activity** Divide the class into groups to prepare presentations on the following topics using pages 20–21 of the Student's Book: • Topic 1: What is genetic engineering and why is it needed? • Topic 2: What is genetic research based on? • Topic 3: What are the arguments in favour of genetic engineering? • Topic 4: What are the arguments against genetic engineering?
5 mins	**Plenary activity** Make sure that each group knows what they have to do to have their presentations ready for the next lesson.

Extension	Reinforcement
Differentiation by outcome should be possible.	Less able students should be in groups where they can be supported.

Homework	Assessment
Finish presentations for next lesson.	N/A
	ICT PowerPoint or other software could be used for the presentations.

LESSON 14: TOPIC 1.10 THE NATURE OF GENETIC ENGINEERING, INCLUDING CLONING

Lesson objectives • To investigate genetic engineering. • To explore why genetic engineering is an important, but controversial, issue.	**Lesson outcomes** By the end of the lesson students should be able to: • explain why genetic engineering is an important, but controversial, issue • explain their own opinion about genetic engineering • explain why some people may disagree with them.
Prior learning • Lesson 13 • Topic 1.6 Human rights in the United Kingdom • Topic 1.8 Why it is important to take part in democratic and electoral processes	**Resources** • Student's Book pages 20–21 • Student group presentations

5 mins	**Starter activity** Students should set up their presentations.
35 mins	**Main activity** 1. Group presentations from lesson 13 on the nature of genetic engineering and non-religious arguments about it, with those students not presenting taking notes. 2. After each presentation students should be given the opportunity to ask the presenters questions, which may lead to some group discussions.
5 mins	**Plenary activity** 1. Make sure everyone has taken notes. 2. Set the homework and read the exam tip on page 21 of the Student's Book.

Extension Differentiation by outcome should be possible.	**Reinforcement** Less able students should be given a photocopy of a more able student's presentation notes.

Homework Set questions **b** and **c** from page 21 of the Student's Book: **b** Do you think cloning should be allowed for medical research? Give two reasons for your point of view. **c** Explain why some people think genetic engineering and cloning for medical research are wrong.	**Assessment** Answers to the homework questions marked according to the Edexcel mark scheme (Appendix 5).
	ICT PowerPoint or other software could be used for the presentations.

LESSON 15: TOPIC 1.11 DIFFERENT ATTITUDES TO GENETIC ENGINEERING AND CLONING IN CHRISTIANITY

Lesson objectives	Lesson outcomes
• To investigate Christian attitudes to genetic engineering. • To explore why there are different attitudes to genetic engineering in Christianity.	By the end of the lesson students should be able to: • explain why there are different attitudes to genetic engineering in Christianity • explain their own opinion about Christian attitudes to genetic engineering • explain why some people may disagree with them.

Prior learning	Resources
Topic 1.10 The nature of genetic engineering, including cloning	Student's Book pages 22–23

15 mins	**Starter activity** Put Starter Sheet 6 on students' desks to complete as soon as they come in. Then have a whole-class discussion on the answers.
25 mins	**Main activity** 1. Put the class into pairs to read pages 22–23 of the Student's Book and answer question **c** from page 23: 'Explain why some Christians allow genetic engineering, but some do not.' 2. Collect answers in for marking.
5 mins	**Plenary activity** 1. Set and discuss the homework question and exam tip on page 23 of the Student's Book. 2. Explain that in the next lesson they will be preparing their revision for the end of section test, therefore they must have their complete files with them.

Extension	Reinforcement
Differentiation by outcome should be possible.	Less able students should be paired with a stronger partner for the main activity.

Homework	Assessment

Set question **d** from page 23 of the Student's Book:
d 'Christians should agree with cloning.'
  i Do you agree? Give reasons for your opinion.
  ii Give reasons why some people may disagree with you.
At least one of the points of view should be Christian with reasons from that religion.
	Answers to the main activity and homework questions marked according to the Edexcel mark scheme (Appendix 5).

	ICT The second part of the starter activity could be done on the interactive whiteboard.

STARTER SHEET 6

Answer Yes or No to the following questions:

1. You have been told you have Huntington's disease and will develop dementia in your 40s and then die. Will you support research using cloning to ensure you do not have children with the disease?

2. You have a four-year-old child with a deadly disease that could be cured if you had another baby so that cells could be cloned from it. Would you have the baby?

3. Do you think genetic research using cloning should be used to produce babies that have physical features chosen by the parents, such as sex, eye colour or hair type?

LESSON 16: REVISION OF SECTION 1

Lesson objectives	**Lesson outcomes**
• To ensure that students have all the resources and information they need to revise Section 1. • To explore the assessment methods and objectives used by Edexcel.	By the end of the lesson students should be able to: • revise Section 1 • answer a test paper on Section 1.

Prior learning	**Resources**
Section 1, lessons 2–15	• Student's Book page 24 • Revision Checklist 1 • Edexcel generic mark scheme (Appendix 5, pages 172–73)

15 mins	**Starter activity** Give out the revision checklist, which students must fill in using their files.
25 mins	**Main activity** Read through 'How to answer exam questions' on page 24 of the Student's Book, relating each answer to the Edexcel generic mark scheme in Appendix 5, pages 172–73.
5 mins	**Plenary activity** Ensure that everyone is prepared for the test in the next lesson.

Extension Differentiation will be achieved by the outcome of the test.	**Reinforcement** Make sure that less able students have help in completing the revision checklist.

Homework Revise for the test.	**Assessment** N/A
	ICT N/A

REVISION CHECKLIST 1

Resources required	Tick if I have it
Key Words Sheet 1.1	
Starter Sheet 2	
Starter Sheet 5	
Notes on the presentations on how Christians make moral decisions	
Notes on the presentations on genetic engineering	
Homework for Topic 1.1: Explain why some Christians use only the Bible when making moral decisions.	
Class work and homework for Topic 1.2: **b** Do you think Christians should use only the teachings of the Church for making moral decisions? Give two reasons for your point of view. **c** Explain why the Church has authority for Christians when making moral decisions.	
Homework for Topic 1.3: 'Your conscience is the best guide for deciding what is right and what is wrong.' **i** Do you agree? Give reasons for your opinion. **ii** Give reasons why some people might disagree with you.	
Homework for Topic 1.4: 'Christians should always do the most loving thing.' **i** Do you agree? Give reasons for your opinion. **ii** Give reasons why some people might disagree with you.	
Homework for Topic 1.5: 'You need more guidance than the Bible when you have to make moral decision.' **i** Do you agree? Give reasons for your opinion. **ii** Give reasons why some people might disagree with you.	
Homework for Topic 1.6: **c** Explain why it is important for the UK to have human rights laws. **d** 'Human Rights laws are only useful for people who break the law.' 　**i** Do you agree? Give reasons for your opinion 　**ii** Give reasons why some people might disagree with you.	
Homework for Topic 1.7: **b** Do you think Christians should accept all human rights laws? Give two reasons for your point of view. **c** Explain why human rights laws are important for Christians.	
Homework for Topic 1.8: 'It doesn't matter whether or not you vote.' **i** Do you agree? Give reasons for your opinion. **ii** Give reasons why some people might disagree with you.	
Homework for Topic 1.9: Explain why the Parable of the Sheep and the Goats leads some Christians to bring about social change.	
Homework for Topic 1.10: **b** Do you think cloning should be allowed for medical research? Give two reasons for your point of view. **c** Explain why some people think genetic engineering and cloning for medical research are wrong.	
Class work and homework for Topic 1.11: **c** Explain why some Christians allow genetic engineering, but some do not. **d** 'Christians should agree with cloning.' 　**i** Do you agree? Give reasons for your opinion. 　**ii** Give reasons why some people might disagree with you.	

LESSON 17: SECTION 1 TEST

Lesson objectives To complete the Section 1 Test in 25 minutes under exam conditions.	**Lesson outcome** By the end of the lesson students should be able to assess how well they have understood Section 1.
Prior learning The whole of Section 1	**Resources** • Section 1 Test • Target setting material (Appendix 7, pages 199–205) • Mark scheme (Appendix 6, pages 174–79)

5 mins	**Starter activity** Hand out the Section 1 Test to the students, explaining what is meant by 'under exam conditions'.
30 mins	**Main activity** 1. Ask the students to complete the questions in 25 minutes. 2. Collect the students' answers.
10 mins	**Plenary activity** Explain the target setting process (material for target setting is provided in Appendix 7, pages 199–202).

Extension The test questions allow differentiation by outcome.	**Reinforcement** Make sure that less able students have a reader or computer if they will be allowed these in the exam.
Homework N/A	**Assessment** Answers to the test marked according to the mark scheme (Appendix 6, pages 174–79).
	ICT N/A

SECTION 1 TEST

Section 1 Religion: Rights and responsibilities

Answer either question 1 or question 2.

1. a) What are human rights? (2 marks)

b) Do you think cloning for medical research is against God's will?

Give two reasons for your point of view. (4 marks)

c) Explain why the Parable of the Sheep and the Goats leads some

Christians to bring about social change. (8 marks)

d) 'Christians should always do the most loving thing.'

(i) Do you agree? Give reasons for your opinion. (3 marks)

(ii) Give reasons why some people may disagree with you. (3 marks)

In your answer you should refer to Christianity.

(Total: 20 marks)

2. a) What is a pressure group? (2 marks)

b) Do you think your conscience is the voice of God?

Give two reasons for your point of view. (4 marks)

c) Explain why it is important for the UK to have human rights laws. (8 marks)

d) 'It doesn't matter whether or not you vote.'

(i) Do you agree? Give reasons for your opinion. (3 marks)

(ii) Give reasons why some people may disagree with you. (3 marks)

(Total: 20 marks)

LESSON 1: TOPIC 2.1 GLOBAL WARMING

Lesson objectives	Lesson outcomes
• To investigate global warming. • To explore the causes and possible solutions to global warming.	By the end of lesson 2, students should be able to: • explain why global warming is happening and how it could be solved • explain their own opinion about global warming • explain why some people may disagree with them.

Prior learning	Resources
Section 1 Religion: Rights and responsibilities	• You will need to book an IT room for this lesson and the next lesson • Student's Book pages 25–28 • Starter Sheet 7

10 mins	**Starter activity** 1. Put Starter Sheet 7 on students' desks or onto the IT network for students to complete on screen. Students should be encouraged to start the task as soon as they sit down. 2. Collect in (or save on the network) the student answers to use at the end of the section to discuss whether the students' expectations were right or wrong.
30 mins	**Main activity** Divide the class into groups of four to write a newspaper article on global warming using pages 26–28 of the Student's Book. The articles need to come to a conclusion about what they think is the true situation.
5 mins	**Plenary activity** Make sure that the groups save what they have done and that they have an action plan on who does what, and how they will complete the articles for next lesson.

Extension	Reinforcement
Differentiation by outcome should be possible.	Less able students should be put into groups with more able students.

Homework	Assessment
Complete the newspaper article for next lesson.	N/A
	ICT The newspaper articles should be completed on a computer using software such as Microsoft Word or Publisher.

STARTER SHEET 7

Name _____ Tutor group _____

Read page 25 of the Student's Book. Using a rating system of 1 (most interesting) to 5 (least interesting), say how interesting you think the topics in this section are going to be.

Topic	Rating
Global warming – its causes and possible solutions	
Forms of pollution and their possible solutions	
Issues connected with the scarcity of natural resources	
Christian teachings on stewardship	
The teachings of one religion other than Christianity on stewardship	
The nature and importance of medical treatments for infertility	
Different attitudes to infertility treatments among Christians	
Attitudes to infertility treatments in one religion other than Christianity	
The nature and importance of transplant surgery	
Different attitudes to transplant surgery in Christianity	
Different attitudes to transplant surgery in one religion other than Christianity	

LESSON 2: TOPIC 2.1 GLOBAL WARMING

Lesson objectives	**Lesson outcomes**
• To investigate global warming. • To explore the causes and possible solutions to global warming.	By the end of the lesson students should be able to: • explain why global warming is happening and how it could be solved • explain their own opinion about global warming • explain why some people may disagree with them.
Prior learning Lesson 1	**Resources** Student's Book pages 26–28

5 mins	**Starter activity** Groups should prepare to present their articles to the class.
35 mins	**Main activity** 1. Each group should present its article to the class. After each presentation, the presenters can take questions from the rest of the class, with students making notes. 2. Print off the two best articles and distribute them to the class.
5 mins	**Plenary activity** Set and discuss the homework, going through the exam tip on page 28 of the Student's Book.

Extension Differentiation by outcome should be possible.	**Reinforcement** Less able students should be informed that they only need to give one reason for the second homework question.
Homework Set questions **b** and **c** from page 28 of the Student's Book. **b** Do you think global warming is a problem? Give two reasons for your point of view. **c** Explain why global warming is happening.	**Assessment** Answers to the homework questions marked according to the Edexcel mark scheme (Appendix 5).
	ICT The newspaper articles could be displayed on an interactive whiteboard.

LESSON 3: TOPIC 2.2 FORMS OF POLLUTION AND THEIR POSSIBLE SOLUTIONS

Lesson objectives	**Lesson outcomes**
• To investigate pollution. • To explore how the problems of pollution may be solved.	By the end of the lesson students should be able to: • explain how the problems of pollution may be solved • explain their own opinion about pollution • explain why some people may disagree with them.
Prior learning Topic 2.1 Global warming	**Resources** • Student's Book pages 29–31 • Starter Sheet 8 • Activity Sheet 1

15 min	**Starter activity** 1. Ask students to complete Starter Sheet 8 as soon as they come in. 2. Make a list of their answers on the board, allowing some discussion as you go through the answers.
20 mins	**Main activity** Put the students into pairs to complete Activity Sheet 1 using pages 29–31 of the Student's Book.
10 mins	**Plenary activity** 1. Go over the answers to the Activity Sheet, encouraging students to amend their answers where necessary. 2. Set and discuss the homework question, going through the exam tip on page 31 of the Student's Book.

Extension Differentiation by outcome should be possible.	**Reinforcement** Make sure the less able students are paired with a more able partner for the main activity.
Homework Set question **c** from page 31 of the Student's Book: Explain how the problems of pollution can be solved.	**Assessment** Answers to the homework question marked according to the Edexcel mark scheme (Appendix 5).
	ICT The starter activity feedback could be done on an interactive whiteboard. Display a blank Starter Sheet on an interactive whiteboard and select students to fill in the blanks with their answers.

STARTER SHEET 8

Fill in the table.

Evidence of pollution you saw on your way to school this morning	How did it get there?
1.	
2.	
3.	
4.	

ACTIVITY SHEET 1

Use pages 29–31 of the Student's Book to answer these questions.

1. Why is acid rain a problem ?	How could it be solved?
2. Why is human waste a problem ?	How could it be solved?
3. Why is eutrophication a problem?	How could it be solved?
4. Why is radioactive pollution a problem?	How could it be solved?

LESSON 4: TOPIC 2.3 THE SCARCITY OF NATURAL RESOURCES

Lesson objectives	Lesson outcomes
• To investigate the scarcity of natural resources. • To explore why the scarcity of natural resources is a threat. • To explore possible solutions.	By the end of the lesson students should be able to: • explain why the scarcity of natural resources is a threat • explain how the threat of scarce natural resources may be solved • explain their own opinion about the scarcity of natural resources • explain why some people may disagree with them.
Prior learning • Topic 2.1 Global warming • Topic 2.2 Forms of pollution and their possible solutions	**Resources** • Student's Book pages 32–33 • Key Words Sheet 2.1

10 mins	**Starter activity** Give the students Key Words Sheet 2.1. Ask them to draw a picture or write a word in the prompt column to help them to remember each word.
30 mins	**Main activity** 1. Display, or distribute a copy of, a brief specimen report to show students what format a report should take (see the section entitled 'How to write a report' at www.howtobooks.co.uk or the pdf file 'How to write reports in plain English' at www.plainenglish.co.uk). 2. Divide the class into pairs. Students should use pages 32–33 of the Student's Book to write a report for the Government on which resources are likely to run out and how the problem could be solved. 3. If time allows, display and discuss one or two of the reports.
5 mins	**Plenary activity** 1. Set the homework question and discuss the exam tip on page 33 of the Student's Book. 2. Inform students that they will have a key words test next lesson.

Extension	Reinforcement
Differentiation by outcome should be possible.	Make sure that the less able students are paired with a stronger partner for the main activity.

Homework	Assessment
Set question **d** from page 33 of the Student's Book: 'Governments will make sure that natural resources do not run out.' **i** Do you agree? Give reasons for your opinion. **ii** Give reasons why some people may disagree with you. In your answer you should refer to at least one religion.	Answers to the homework question marked according to the Edexcel mark scheme (Appendix 5).
	ICT • The reports could be written on a computer using a report-writing template. • The reports could be displayed on an interactive whiteboard.

KEY WORDS SHEET 2.1

Key Word	Meaning	Your Prompt
artificial insemination	injecting semen into the uterus by artificial means	
conservation	protecting and preserving natural resources and the environment	
creation	the act of creating the universe, or the universe which has been created	
embryo	a fertilised egg in the first eight weeks after conception	
environment	the surroundings in which plants and animals live and on which they depend to continue living	
global warming	the increase in the temperature of the Earth's atmosphere (thought to be caused by the greenhouse effect)	
infertility	not being able to have children	
in-vitro fertilisation	the method of fertilising a human egg in a test tube	
natural resources	naturally occurring materials, such as oil and fertile land, which can be used by humans	
organ donation	giving organs to be used in transplant surgery	
stewardship	looking after something so it can be passed on to the next generation	
surrogacy	an arrangement whereby a woman bears a child on behalf of another woman or where an egg is donated and fertilised by the husband through IVF and then implanted into the wife's uterus	

LESSON 5: TOPIC 2.4 CHRISTIAN TEACHINGS ON STEWARDSHIP

Lesson objectives	Lesson outcomes
• To investigate Christian teachings on stewardship. • To explore how Christian teachings on stewardship affect Christian attitudes to the environment.	By the end of the lesson students should be able to: • explain how Christian teachings about stewardship may affect their attitudes to the environment • explain their own opinion about Christian teachings on stewardship • explain why some people may disagree with them.
Prior learning	**Resources**
• Topic 2.1 Global warming • Topic 2.2 Forms of pollution and their possible solutions • Topic 2.3 The scarcity of natural resources	• Student's Book pages 34–35 • Key Words Sheet 2.2

10 mins	**Starter activity** 1. Give out Key Words Sheet 2.2 for students to complete individually. 2. Collect them in for marking.
35 mins	**Main activity** 1. Read through pages 34–35 of the Student's Book with the class, allowing plenty of discussion. 2. Display 'Reasons why Christians should help conserve the environment' on the board and ask students to come up and write a reason on the board. 3. Ask students to copy the list, or print it off and give a copy to each student.
5 mins	**Plenary activity** Set the homework question and discuss the exam tip on page 35 of the Student's Book.

Extension	Reinforcement
• Differentiation by outcome should be possible. • Students could be set question **d** from page 35 of the Student's Book as extra homework: 'If Christians followed their teachings on stewardship, there would be no environmental problems.' i Do you agree? Give reasons for your opinion. ii Give reasons why some people may disagree with you. At least one of the points of view should be Christian with reasons from that religion.	Make sure that less able students have a copy of the list of reasons and are not called up to write on the board unless they volunteer.

Homework	Assessment
Set question **b** from page 35 of the Student's Book: Do you think Christians should do more to care for the environment? Give two reasons for your point of view.	• Marking of Key Words Sheet 2.2. • Answers to the homework question marked according to the Edexcel mark scheme (Appendix 5).
	ICT The main activity, parts 2 and 3, could be done on an interactive whiteboard.

KEY WORDS SHEET 2.2

Fill in the blanks in the table.

Key Word	Meaning
artificial insemination	
conservation	
	the act of creating the universe, or the universe which has been created
	a fertilised egg in the first eight weeks after conception
environment	
global warming	
	not being able to have children
	the method of fertilising a human egg in a test tube
	naturally occurring materials, such as oil and fertile land, which can be used by humans
organ donation	
	looking after something so it can be passed on to the next generation
surrogacy	

LESSON 6: TOPIC 2.5 THE TEACHINGS OF ONE RELIGION OTHER THAN CHRISTIANITY ON STEWARDSHIP

Lesson objectives	Lesson outcomes
• To investigate teachings on stewardship in one religion other than Christianity. • To explore how these teachings on stewardship affect the attitudes to the environment of the followers of the religion.	By the end of the lesson students should be able to: • explain how the teachings on stewardship in one religion other than Christianity affect the attitudes to the environment of the followers of the religion • explain their own opinion about the teachings on stewardship of one religion other than Christianity • explain why some people may disagree with them.
Prior learning	Resources
• Topic 2.1 Global warming • Topic 2.2 Forms of pollution and their possible solutions • Topic 2.3 The scarcity of natural resources	• Student's Book pages 36–37, 38–39, 40–41 or 42–43 • Starter Sheet 9

15 mins	**Starter activity** 1. Ask students to complete Starter Sheet 9 as soon as they come in. 2. Take feedback from the students and write their ideas on the board.
20 mins	**Main activity** 1. Read through pages 36–37 (Islam), pages 38–39 (Judaism), pages 40–41 (Hinduism) or pages 42–43 (Sikhism) of the Student's Book. 2. Allow plenty of discussion about the teachings on stewardship and the effects on believers' attitudes to the environment. Where possible, point out the similarities with Christian attitudes.
10 mins	**Plenary activity** 1. Return to the ideas from the starter activity and discuss whether Muslims/Jews/Hindus/Sikhs would have a duty to care for any of these things. 2. Explain and set the homework, making sure to discuss the exam tip on page 37/39/41/43.

Extension	Reinforcement
Differentiation by outcome should be possible.	Less able students could be advised that they only need to give two reasons for the homework question.

Homework	Assessment
Set question **c** from page 37/39/41/43 of the Student's Book depending on the religion being studied: Choose one religion other than Christianity and explain why its followers have a duty to take care of the Earth.	Answers to the homework question marked according to the Edexcel mark scheme (Appendix 5).
	ICT The starter feedback could be displayed on an interactive whiteboard. Select students to enter their ideas on the Starter Sheet.

STARTER SHEET 9

Things you need to take care of in your life	Things your parents need to take care of in their lives

LESSON 7: TOPIC 2.6 THE NATURE AND IMPORTANCE OF MEDICAL TREATMENTS FOR INFERTILITY

Lesson objectives	Lesson outcomes
• To investigate medical treatments for infertility. • To explore why medical treatments for infertility are important.	By the end of lesson 8 students should be able to: • explain why medical treatments for infertility are important • explain their own opinion about medical treatments for infertility • explain why some people may disagree with them.

Prior learning	Resources
Section 1, Topics 1.1–1.5 Christian moral decision-making	• Student's Book pages 44–45 • This lesson must take place in the computer room, so book in advance.

15 mins	**Starter activity**
	1. In pairs, students should use the internet to find definitions of:
	  • in-vitro fertilisation (IVF)
	  • artificial insemination by husband (AIH)
	  • artificial insemination by donor (AID)
	  • egg donation
	  • embryo donation
	  • surrogacy.
	2. Students should check their answers against page 44 of the Student's Book and amend where necessary – their answers should be kept in their file.

25 mins	**Main activity** In pairs, students should prepare a presentation based on pages 44–45 of the Student's Book (using PowerPoint, Publisher or other relevant software). They will give their presentation to the class in the next lesson. The presentation should cover: • why infertility treatments are important • which infertility treatments are going to give the best result with the fewest problems.
5 mins	**Plenary activity** Check that each pair knows who is going to do what to make sure that they have their presentations ready for the next lesson.

Extension	Reinforcement
Differentiation by outcome should be possible.	Less able students should be paired with a more able partner.

Homework	Assessment
Complete the presentations.	N/A
	ICT • The starter activity involves searching the internet for information. • PowerPoint or other software could be used for the presentations.

LESSON 8: TOPIC 2.6 THE NATURE AND IMPORTANCE OF MEDICAL TREATMENTS FOR INFERTILITY

Lesson objectives	Lesson outcomes
• To investigate medical treatments for infertility. • To explore why medical treatments for infertility are important.	By the end of the lesson students should be able to: • explain why medical treatments for infertility are important • explain their own opinion about medical treatments for infertility • explain why some people may disagree with them.
Prior learning • Lesson 7 • Section 1, topics 1.1–1.5 Christian moral decision-making	**Resources** • Student's Book pages 44–45 • Students' presentations • Four copies of Homework Sheet 2 for each student

5 mins	**Starter activity** Students should set up their presentations.
35 mins	**Main activity** 1. Group presentations from lesson 7 on infertility treatments, with those students not presenting taking notes. 2. After each presentation students should be given the opportunity to ask the presenters questions, which may lead to some group discussions.
5 mins	**Plenary activity** Set and explain the questionnaire homework.

Extension	Reinforcement
Differentiation by outcome should be possible.	• Make sure less able students are paired with a more able partner and are given photocopies of good notes on the presentations. • If possible set aside a time before the next lesson when you can help them to fill in the tally charts based on their completed questionnaires.

Homework	Assessment
Tell students to give out the questionnaire on infertility treatments to four adults (if possible a Catholic, a non-Catholic Christian, a member of another religion, a person with no religion) and bring the completed sheets to the next lesson.	N/A
	ICT PowerPoint or other software could be used for the presentations.

HOMEWORK SHEET 2

Questionnaire on attitudes to infertility treatments

As part of my GCSE Religious Studies course, I am studying religious and non-religious attitudes to fertility treatments. I would be grateful if you could spare a few moments to answer these questions. Please tick the box which most applies to you.

1. What is your religion?

   Roman Catholic ☐

   Other Christian ☐

   Islam ☐

   Judaism ☐

   Hinduism ☐

   Sikhism ☐

   No religion ☐

2. Do you think IVF (test-tube babies) should be available on the NHS?

   Yes ☐

   No ☐

   Not sure ☐

3. Do you think AID (using sperm from an unknown man) should be available on the NHS?

   Yes ☐

   No ☐

   Not sure ☐

4. Do you think egg donation (using an egg from an unknown woman) should be available on the NHS?

   Yes ☐

   No ☐

   Not sure ☐

5. Do you think embryo donation (using egg and sperm from unknown people for test-tube babies) should be available on the NHS?

   Yes ☐

   No ☐

   Not sure ☐

6. Do you think surrogacy (when the sperm and egg of the mother and father are fertilised by IVF and then placed in another woman's womb) should be available on the NHS?

   Yes ☐

   No ☐

   Not sure ☐

LESSON 9: TOPIC 2.7 DIFFERENT ATTITUDES TO INFERTILITY TREATMENTS AMONG CHRISTIANS

Lesson objectives • To investigate different Christian attitudes to infertility treatments. • To explore why there are different attitudes to infertility treatments in Christianity.	**Lesson outcomes** By the end of the lesson students should be able to: • explain why there are different attitudes to infertility treatments in Christianity • explain their own opinion about Christian attitudes to infertility treatments • explain why some people may disagree with them.
Prior learning Topic 2.6 The nature and importance of medical treatments for infertility	**Resources** • Student's Book pages 46–47 • Starter Sheet 10 • Activity Sheet 2 • Activity Sheet 3

10 mins	**Starter activity** Display the blank tally charts (Starter Sheet 10) on the board and fill them in using the results of students' questionnaires. Make sure a copy of the final results is kept to use in the next lesson.
30 mins	**Main activity** 1. In pairs students should fill in Activity Sheets 2 and 3 using pages 46–47 of the Student's Book. 2. Compare the questionnaire results for Catholics and other Christians with students' answers to the Activity Sheets. Allow plenty of discussion.
5 mins	**Plenary activity** Set and discuss the homework question.

Extension Differentiation by outcome should be possible.	**Reinforcement** Make sure less able students are paired with a stronger partner for the main activity and are advised that they only need to give one reason for each part of their homework answer.
Homework Set question **d** from page 47 of the Student's Book: All Christians should raise a family. i Do you agree? Give reasons for your opinion. ii Give reasons why some people may disagree with you. In your answer, you should refer to Christianity.	**Assessment** Answers to the homework question marked according to the Edexcel mark scheme (Appendix 5).
	ICT The tally chart could be filled in on an interactive whiteboard.

STARTER SHEET 10
FERTILITY TREATMENT QUESTIONNAIRE – TALLY CHARTS

'Yes' answers

	Question 1	Question 2	Question 3	Question 4	Question 5	Question 6
Roman Catholic						
Other Christian						
Islam						
Judaism						
Hinduism						
Sikhism						
No religion						

'No' answers

	Question 1	Question 2	Question 3	Question 4	Question 5	Question 6
Roman Catholic						
Other Christian						
Islam						
Judaism						
Hinduism						
Sikhism						
No religion						

'Not sure' answers

	Question 1	Question 2	Question 3	Question 4	Question 5	Question 6
Roman Catholic						
Other Christian						
Islam						
Judaism						
Hinduism						
Sikhism						
No religion						

ACTIVITY SHEET 2

Use pages 46–47 of the Student's Book to fill in the blank spaces in this table.

Infertility treatment	Would Catholic Christians agree with it?	Why?
In-vitro fertilisation (IVF)		
Artificial insemination by husband (AIH)		
Artificial insemination by donor (AID)		
Egg donation		
Embryo donation		
Surrogacy		

ACTIVITY SHEET 3

Use pages 46–47 of the Student's Book to fill in the blank spaces in this table.

Infertility treatment	Would non-Catholic Christians agree with it?	Why?
In-vitro fertilisation (IVF)		
Artificial insemination by husband (AIH)		
Artificial insemination by donor (AID)		
Egg donation		
Embryo donation		
Surrogacy		

LESSON 10: TOPIC 2.8 ATTITUDES TO INFERTILITY TREATMENTS IN ONE RELIGION OTHER THAN CHRISTIANITY

Lesson objectives • To investigate different attitudes to infertility treatments in one religion other than Christianity. • To explore why there are different attitudes to infertility treatments in one religion other than Christianity.	**Lesson outcomes** By the end of the lesson students should be able to: • explain why there are different attitudes to infertility treatments in one religion other than Christianity • explain their own opinion about the attitudes to infertility treatments in one religion other than Christianity • explain why some people may disagree with them.
Prior learning • Topic 2.6 The nature and importance of medical treatments for infertility • Topic 2.7 Different attitudes to infertility treatments among Christians	**Resources** • Student's Book page 48, 49, 50 or 51 • Activity Sheet 4 • Paper and sticky tape

15 mins	**Starter activity** 1. Write this question on the board: 'If you were married and having difficulty having a baby, what would you do?' 2. Ask students to write their answers on a piece of A4 and to stick them on the board. 3. Read out and discuss a selection of the answers.
25 mins	**Main activity** 1. In pairs, students should fill in Activity Sheet 4 using Student's Book page 48 (Islam), page 49 (Judaism), page 50 (Hinduism) or page 51 (Sikhism). 2. Compare the questionnaire results for Muslims/Jews/Hindus/Sikhs with students' answers to the Activity Sheet. Allow plenty of discussion. 3. Compare the final results of the questionnaire tally with their answers to the Activity Sheets. Allow plenty of discussion.
5 mins	**Plenary activity** Discuss and set the homework, discussing the exam tip on page 48/49/50/51 of the Student's Book.

Extension • Differentiation by outcome should be possible. • More able students could be set question **d** from page 48/49/50/51 of the Student's Book as an extra homework: 'Religious people have no greater right to have children than non-religious people.' i Do you agree? Give reasons for your opinion. ii Give reasons why some people may disagree with you. In your answer, you should refer to at least one religion.	**Reinforcement** Less able students should be paired with a more able partner for the paired activities and should be advised they only need to give one reason for each attitude.

Homework Set question **c** from page 48/49/50/51 of the Student's Book depending on the religion being studied: Choose one religion other than Christianity and explain why its followers agree with some infertility treatments but not others.	**Assessment** Answers to the homework question marked according to the Edexcel mark scheme (Appendix 5).
	ICT The starter activity and tally chart could be presented and analysed on an interactive whiteboard.

ACTIVITY SHEET 4

Use page 48/49/50/51 of the Student's Book, depending on the religion you are studying, to fill in the blank spaces in this table.

Infertility treatment	Would Muslims/Jews/Hindus/Sikhs agree with it?	Why?
In-vitro fertilisation (IVF)		
Artificial insemination by husband (AIH)		
Artificial insemination by donor (AID)		
Egg donation		
Embryo donation		
Surrogacy		

LESSON 11: TOPIC 2.9 THE NATURE AND IMPORTANCE OF TRANSPLANT SURGERY

Lesson objectives • To investigate transplant surgery. • To explore why transplant surgery is important.	**Lesson outcomes** By the end of the lesson students should be able to: • explain why transplant surgery is important • explain their own opinion about transplant surgery • explain why some people may disagree with them.
Prior learning • Topic 2.6 The nature and importance of medical treatments for infertility • Topic 2.7 Different attitudes to infertility treatments among Christians • Topic 2.8 Attitudes to infertility treatments in one religion other than Christianity	**Resources** Student's Book pages 52–53

15 mins	**Starter activity** 1. In pairs, or groups of four, students should answer the question 'Why do transplants from dead donors raise more problems than transplants from live donors?' 2. Discuss their answers.
25 mins	**Main activity** Read through pages 52–53 of the Student's Book, with plenty of discussion. If any students offer arguments against transplant surgery, make sure that all students take notes.
5 mins	**Plenary activity** Set and discuss the homework.

Extension • Differentiation by outcome should be possible. • Set question **c** from page 53 of the Student's Book as an extra homework question: Explain why many people believe transplant surgery is important.	**Reinforcement** Less able students should be paired with a more able partner for the starter activity.
Homework • Set question **b** from page 53 of the Student's Book: Do you think transplant surgery is worth the expense? Give two reasons for your point of view. • Revise the key words for a test next lesson.	**Assessment** Answers to the homework question marked according to the Edexcel mark scheme (Appendix 5).
	ICT The starter activity is best done on an interactive whiteboard so that a final version can be printed off and given to every student.

LESSON 12: TOPIC 2.10 DIFFERENT ATTITUDES TO TRANSPLANT SURGERY IN CHRISTIANITY

Lesson objectives	Lesson outcomes
• To investigate different Christian attitudes to transplant surgery. • To explore why there are different attitudes to transplant surgery in Christianity.	By the end of lesson 13 students should be able to: • explain why there are different attitudes to transplant surgery in Christianity • explain their own opinion about Christian attitudes to transplant surgery • explain why some people may disagree with them.

Prior learning	Resources
Topic 2.9 The nature and importance of transplant surgery	• Student's Book pages 54–55 • Key Word Sheet 2.3

10 mins	**Starter activity** 1. Put Key Words Sheet 2.3 on students' desks to complete as soon as they sit down. 2. Collect it in for marking.
30 mins	**Main activity** Divide the class into groups to prepare presentations, using pages 54–55 of the Student's Book, on the following topics: • Topic 1: Why most Christians agree with transplant surgery as long as donors are not paid • Topic 2: Why some Christians only agree with transplants from living patients who have not been paid • Topic 3: Why some Christians do not accept any form of transplant surgery.
5 mins	**Plenary activity** Make sure that each group knows what they have to do to have their presentations ready for the next lesson.

Extension	Reinforcement
Differentiation by outcome should be possible.	Less able students should be placed in a group with more able students.

Homework	Assessment
Finish presentations for the next lesson.	Marking the key words test.
	ICT PowerPoint or other software could be used for the presentations.

KEY WORDS SHEET 2.3

Fill in the blanks in the table.

Key Word	Meaning
	injecting semen into the uterus by artificial means
	protecting and preserving natural resources and the environment
	the act of creating the universe, or the universe which has been created
	a fertilised egg in the first eight weeks after conception
	the surroundings in which plants and animals live and on which they depend to live
	the increase in the temperature of the Earth's atmosphere (thought to be caused by the greenhouse effect)
	not being able to have children
	the method of fertilising a human egg in a test tube
	naturally occurring materials, such as oil and fertile land, which can be used by humans
	giving organs to be used in transplant surgery
	looking after something so it can be passed on to the next generation
	an arrangement whereby a woman bears a child on behalf of another woman or where an egg is donated and fertilised by the husband through IVF and then implanted into the wife's uterus

LESSON 13: TOPIC 2.10 DIFFERENT ATTITUDES TO TRANSPLANT SURGERY IN CHRISTIANITY

Lesson objectives	Lesson outcomes
• To investigate different Christian attitudes to transplant surgery. • To explore why there are different attitudes to transplant surgery in Christianity.	By the end of the lesson students should be able to: • explain why there are different attitudes to transplant surgery in Christianity • explain their own opinion about Christian attitudes to transplant surgery • explain why some people may disagree with them.
Prior learning • Lesson 12 • Topic 2.9 The nature and importance of transplant surgery	**Resources** Student's Book pages 54–55

5 mins	**Starter activity** Students should set up their presentations.
35 mins	**Main activity** 1. Group presentations from lesson 12 on Christian attitudes to transplant surgery, with those students not presenting taking notes. 2. After each presentation students should be given the opportunity to ask the presenters questions, which may lead to some group discussions.
5 mins	**Plenary activity** Set and explain the homework, discussing the exam focus from page 7 of the Student's Book.

Extension	Reinforcement
Differentiation by outcome should be possible.	Less able students should be placed in a group with more able students.

Homework	Assessment
Set question **d** from page 53 of the Student's Book: 'People should be able to sell their organs for transplant.' **i** Do you agree? Give reasons for your opinion. **ii** Give reasons why some people may disagree with you. In your answer, you should refer to at least one religion.	Answers to the homework question marked according to the Edexcel mark scheme (Appendix 5).
	ICT PowerPoint or other software could be used for the presentations.

LESSON 14: TOPIC 2.11 DIFFERENT ATTITUDES TO TRANSPLANT SURGERY IN ONE RELIGION OTHER THAN CHRISTIANITY

Lesson objectives	Lesson outcomes
• To investigate different attitudes to transplant surgery in one religion other than Christianity. • To explore why there are different attitudes to transplant surgery in one religion other than Christianity.	By the end of the lesson students should be able to: • explain why there are different attitudes to transplant surgery in one religion other than Christianity • explain their own opinion about attitudes to transplant surgery in one religion other than Christianity • explain why some people may disagree with them.
Prior learning Topic 2.9 The nature and importance of transplant surgery	**Resources** Student's Book page 56, 57, 58 or 59

15 mins	**Starter activity** 1. Write this question on the board: 'The UK government is considering a bill that would assume all UK residents are organ donors unless they specifically opt out. Do you think this is a good idea? Give two reasons.' Ask students to write down their reasons. 2. Use their answers to work out a class decision. 3. Discuss the reasons for and against the proposal.
25 mins	**Main activity** 1. Read and discuss the exam tip on page 56 (Islam), page 57 (Judaism), page 58 (Hinduism) or page 59 (Sikhism) of the Student's Book. 2. Put students in pairs to answer question **c**: Choose one religion other than Christianity and explain why some of its followers agree with transplant surgery and some do not. 3. Collect students' answers in for marking, then either look at the photo and discus the caption for Islam/Judaism/Hinduism or discuss the margin quotes for Sikhism.
5 mins	**Plenary activity** 1. Set and discuss the homework question. 2. Explain that in the next lesson they will be preparing their revision for the end of section test, therefore they must have their complete files with them.

Extension	Reinforcement
Differentiation by outcome should be possible.	Less able students should be paired with a more able student for the main activity.

Homework	Assessment
Set question **d** from page 56/57/58/59 of the Student's Book: 'All religious people should carry a donor card.' i Do you agree? Give reasons for your opinion. ii Give reasons why some people may disagree with you. In your answer, you should refer to at least one religion.	Answers to the main activity and homework questions marked according to the Edexcel mark scheme (Appendix 5).
	ICT The answers to the starter activity could be recorded and analysed on an interactive whiteboard.

LESSON 15: REVISION OF SECTION 2

Lesson objectives • To ensure that students have all the resources and information they need to revise Section 2. • To explore the assessment methods and objectives used by Edexcel.	**Lesson outcomes** By the end of the lesson students should be able to: • revise Section 2 • answer a test paper on Section 2.
Prior learning Section 2, lessons 1–14	**Resources** • Student's Book page 60 • Revision Checklist 2 • Edexcel generic mark scheme (Appendix 5, pages 172–73) • Completed Starter Sheet 1

20 mins	**Starter activity** 1. Display the students' answers to Starter Sheet 7 from lesson 1 and discuss whether the students' expectations were right or wrong. 2. Give out the revision checklist, which students must fill in using their files.
20 mins	**Main activity** Read through 'How to answer exam questions' on page 60 of the Student's Book, relating each answer to the Edexcel generic mark scheme in Appendix 5, pages 172–73.
5 mins	**Plenary activity** Ensure that everyone is prepared for the test in the next lesson.

Extension Differentiation will be achieved by the outcomes of the test.	**Reinforcement** Make sure that less able students have help in completing the revision checklist.
Homework Revise for the test.	**Assessment** N/A
	ICT N/A

REVISION CHECKLIST 2

Resources required	Tick if I have it
Key Words Sheet 2.1	
Two articles on global warming	
Activity Sheet 1	
Activity Sheet 2	
Activity Sheet 3	
Activity Sheet 4	
Report on resources	
List of reasons for Christians conserving the environment	
Notes on infertility treatment presentations	
Infertility treatments questionnaire tally chart	
Notes on Christian attitudes to transplants presentations	
Homework for Topic 2.1: b Do you think global warming is a problem? Give two reasons for your point of view. c Explain why global warming is happening.	
Homework for Topic 2.2: Explain how the problems of pollution can be solved.	
Homework for Topic 2.3: 'Governments will make sure that natural resources do not run out.' i Do you agree? Give reasons for your opinion. ii Give reasons why some people may disagree with you.	
Homework for Topic 2.4: Do you think Christians should do more to care for the environment? Give two reasons for your point of view.	
Homework for Topic 2.5: Choose one religion other than Christianity and explain why its followers have a duty to take care of the Earth.	
Homework for Topic 2.7: 'All Christians should raise a family.' i Do you agree? Give reasons for your opinion. ii Give reasons why some people may disagree with you.	
Homework for Topic 2.8: Choose one religion other than Christianity and explain why its followers agree with some infertility treatments but not others.	
Homework for Topic 2.9: Do you think transplant surgery is worth the expense? Give two reasons for your point of view.	
Homework for Topic 2.10: 'People should be able to sell their organs for transplant.' i Do you agree? Give reasons for your opinion. ii Give reasons why some people may disagree with you.	
Homework for Topic 2.11: 'All religious people should carry a donor card.' i Do you agree? Give reasons for your opinion. ii Give reasons why some people may disagree with you.	

LESSON 16: SECTION 2 TEST

Lesson objectives To complete the Section 2 Test in 25 minutes under exam conditions.	**Lesson outcome** By the end of the lesson students should be able to assess how well they have understood Section 2.
Prior learning The whole of Section 2	**Resources** • Section 2 Test • Target setting material (Appendix 7, pages 199–201, 203) • Mark scheme (Appendix 6, pages 180–85)

5 mins	**Starter activity** Hand out the Section 2 Test to the students, explaining what is meant by 'under exam conditions'.
30 mins	**Main activity** 1. Ask the students to complete the questions in 25 minutes. 2. Collect the students' answers.
10 mins	**Plenary activity** Explain the target setting process (material for target setting is provided in Appendix 7, pages 199–202)

Extension The test questions allow differentiation by outcome.	**Reinforcement** Make sure that less able students have a reader or computer if they will be allowed these in the exam.
Homework N/A	**Assessment** Answers to the test marked according to the mark scheme (Appendix 6, pages 180–85).
	ICT N/A

SECTION 2 TEST

Section 2 Religion: Environmental and medical issues

Answer either question 1 or question 2.

1. a) What is organ donation? (2 marks)

b) Do you think children born from sperm or egg donation have a right to know the donors?

Give two reasons for your point of view. (4 marks)

c) Choose one religion other than Christianity and explain why its followers agree with some infertility treatments but not others. (8 marks)

d) 'If Christians followed their teachings on stewardship, there would be no environmental problems.'

(i) Do you agree? Give reasons for your opinion. (3 marks)

(ii) Give reasons why some people may disagree with you. (3 marks)

In your answer you should refer to at least one religion.

(Total: 20 marks)

2. a) What is surrogacy? (2 marks)

b) Do you think global warming is a problem?

Give two reasons for your point of view. (4 marks)

c) Choose one religion other than Christianity and explain why its followers have a duty to take care of the earth. (8 marks)

d) 'All Christian have a right to have children.'

(i) Do you agree? Give reasons for your opinion. (3 marks)

(ii) Give reasons why some people may disagree with you. (3 marks)

In your answer you should refer to at least one religion.

(Total: 20 marks)

LESSON 1: TOPIC 3.1 THE UNITED NATIONS AND WORLD PEACE

Lesson objectives	**Lesson outcomes**
• To investigate the United Nations and world peace. • To explore how and why the United Nations works for world peace.	By the end of lesson 2 students should be able to: • explain how and why the United Nations works for world peace • explain their own opinion about the United Nations and world peace • explain why some people may disagree with them.

Prior learning	**Resources**
• Section 1 Religion: Rights and responsibilities • Section 2 Religion: Environmental and medical issues	• Student's Book pages 61–64 • Sticky notes

5 mins	**Starter activity** Ask students to read the introduction to section 3 on page 61 of the Student's Book and to write on a sticky note which they think will be the most interesting topic. Students should be encouraged to start the task as soon as they sit down.

40 mins	**Main activity**
	1. Display the sticky notes from the starter activity and work out which the class thinks will be the most interesting topic. Keep a record of this to use in lesson 15.
	2. Divide the class into groups to prepare presentations on the following topics using pages 62–64 of the Student's Book:
	  • Topic 1: What the UN is and why it was set up
	  • Topic 2: Why the UN is important for world peace
	  • Topic 3: One example of the UN's work for world peace.

5 mins	**Plenary activity** Check that each group knows who is going to do what to make sure that they have their presentations ready for the next lesson.

Extension Differentiation by outcome should be possible.	**Reinforcement** Less able students should be in groups where they can be supported.
Homework Complete the presentations.	**Assessment** N/A
	ICT PowerPoint or other software could be used for the presentations.

LESSON 2: TOPIC 3.1 THE UNITED NATIONS AND WORLD PEACE

Lesson objectives	**Lesson outcomes**
• To investigate the United Nations and world peace. • To explore how and why the United Nations works for world peace.	By the end of the lesson students should be able to: • explain how and why the United Nations works for world peace • explain their own opinion about the United Nations and world peace • explain why some people may disagree with them.
Prior learning	**Resources**
• Section 3, lesson 1 • Section 1 Religion: Rights and responsibilities • Section 2 Religion: Environmental and medical issues	• Student's Book pages 62–64 • Student presentations

5 mins	**Starter activity** Students should set up their presentations.
35 mins	**Main activity** 1. Group presentations from lesson 1 on the work of the UN, with those students not presenting taking notes. 2. After each presentation students should be given the opportunity to ask the presenters questions, which may lead to some group discussions.
5 mins	**Plenary activity** Set and discuss the homework questions using the exam tip from page 64 of the Student's Book.

Extension Differentiation by outcome should be possible.	**Reinforcement** • Make sure that less able students are given photocopies of a more able student's presentation notes. • They should only be given the first homework question.

Homework Set questions **b** and **d** from page 64 of the Student's Book: **b** Do you think the United Nations is important? Give two reasons for your point of view. **d** 'The United Nations is the best chance for world peace.' i Do you agree? Give reasons for your opinion. ii Give reasons why some people may disagree with you. In your answer, you should refer to at least one religion.	**Assessment** Answers to the homework questions marked according to the Edexcel mark scheme (Appendix 5).
	ICT PowerPoint or other software could be used for the presentations.

LESSON 3: TOPIC 3.2 HOW RELIGIOUS ORGANISATIONS TRY TO PROMOTE WORLD PEACE

Lesson objectives
- To investigate religious organisations and world peace.
- To explore how religious organisations work for world peace.

Lesson outcomes
By the end of the lesson students should be able to:
- explain how religious organisations work for world peace
- explain their own opinion about religious organisations and world peace
- explain why some people may disagree with them.

Prior learning
Topic 3.1 The United Nations and world peace

Resources
- Student's Book page 65
- Key Words Sheet 3.1
- Video clip on the work of a religious organisation

10 mins	**Starter activity** Give the students Key Words Sheet 3.1. Ask them to draw a picture or write a word in the prompt column to help them to remember each word.
30 mins	**Main activity** 1. Show a video on the work of a religious organisation (for example, at www.ikvpaxchristi.nl/UK/ you will find a video about the peace and sports programme in the border area between Sudan, Ethiopia, Kenya and Uganda). Up-to-date news and videos about the work of Pax Christi can be found on www.ikvpaxchristi.nl/UK/. 2. Discuss the value and importance of the work. 3. Read through page 65 of the Student's Book, with plenty of discussion.
5 mins	**Plenary activity** Set the homework and discuss the exam tip on page 65 of the Student's Book.

Extension
Students could be asked to research two other activities of Pax Christi using www.ikvpaxchristi.nl/UK/ and discuss their value for world peace.

Reinforcement
Less able students should only be set one of the homework questions.

Homework
Set questions **b** and **c** from page 65 of the Student's Book:
b Do you think religious organisations can stop wars? Give two reasons for your point of view.
c Explain how religious organisations work for world peace.

Assessment
Answers to the homework questions marked according to the Edexcel mark scheme (Appendix 5).

ICT
- If sufficient computers are available students could find the video themselves and watch it from the internet.
- More able students should use the internet for their extension work.

KEY WORDS SHEET 3.1

Key Word	Meaning	Your Prompt
aggression	attacking without being provoked	
bullying	intimidating/frightening people weaker than yourself	
conflict resolution	bringing a fight or struggle to a peaceful conclusion	
exploitation	taking advantage of a weaker group	
forgiveness	the act of stopping blaming someone and/or pardoning them for what they have done wrong	
just war	a war that is fought for the right reasons and in a right way	
pacifism	the belief that all disputes should be settled by peaceful means	
reconciliation	bringing together people who were opposed to each other	
respect	treating a person or their feelings with consideration	
the United Nations	an international body set up to promote world peace and co-operation	
weapons of mass destruction	weapons which can destroy large areas and numbers of people	
world peace	the ending of war throughout the whole world (the basic aim of the United Nations)	

LESSON 4: TOPIC 3.3 WHY WARS OCCUR

Lesson objectives • To investigate current conflicts in the world. • To explore why wars occur.	**Lesson outcomes** By the end of lesson 5 students should be able to: • explain why wars occur using examples from current conflicts • explain their own opinion about why wars occur • explain why some people may disagree with them.
Prior learning • Topic 3.1 The United Nations and world peace • Topic 3.2 How religious organisations try to promote world peace	**Resources** • Student's Book pages 66–67 • Video clip on the Afghan war

15 mins	**Starter activity** 1. Show a brief video clip of the Afghan war from a source such as www.newsdaily.com/video, which has plenty of news video clips and is updated daily. 2. Discuss the class's feelings about the video.
25 mins	**Main activity** Divide the class into pairs to prepare presentations on one of the following topics using pages 66–67 of the Student's Book: • Topic 1: How religion causes wars • Topic 2: How nationalism and ethnicity cause wars • Topic 3: How economics causes wars • Topic 4: How ideological differences cause wars (this should be a more able group and they should have internet access at home to research additional information).
5 mins	**Plenary activity** Check that each pair knows who is going to do what to make sure they have their presentations ready for the next lesson.

Extension Differentiation by outcome should be possible.	**Reinforcement** Less able students should be given topic 1, 2 or 3 and should be paired with a more able partner.

Homework Complete the presentations.	**Assessment** N/A
	ICT • PowerPoint or other software could be used for the presentations. • The video clip should be shown via the internet using an interactive whiteboard or data projector.

LESSON 5: TOPIC 3.3 WHY WARS OCCUR

Lesson objectives	Lesson outcomes
• To investigate current conflicts in the world. • To explore why wars occur.	By the end of the lesson students should be able to: • explain why wars occur using examples from current conflicts • explain their own opinion about why wars occur • explain why some people may disagree with them.
Prior learning • Lesson 4 • Topic 3.1 The United Nations and world peace • Topic 3.2 How religious organisations try to promote world peace	**Resources** • Student's Book pages 66–67 • Student presentations

5 mins	**Starter activity** Students should set up their presentations.
35 mins	**Main activity** 1. Group presentations from lesson 4 on why wars occur, with those students not presenting taking notes. 2. After each presentation students should be given the opportunity to ask the presenters questions, which may lead to some group discussions.
5 mins	**Plenary activity** Set and discuss the homework question using the exam tip on page 67 of the Student's Book.

Extension	Reinforcement
• Differentiation by outcome should be possible. • Students placed in group 4 would be more extended by their research.	Make sure that less able students are given photocopies of a more able student's presentation notes.

Homework	Assessment

• Set question **d** from page 67 of the Student's Book:
'Religion is the main cause of wars.'
  i Do you agree? Give reasons for your opinion.
  ii Give reasons why some people may disagree with you.
• Ask students to revise for a key words test in the next lesson.
	Answers to the homework question marked according to the Edexcel mark scheme (Appendix 5).

	ICT Presentations could be done on PowerPoint, Publisher or similar software.

LESSON 6: TOPIC 3.4 THE NATURE AND IMPORTANCE OF THE THEORY OF JUST WAR

Lesson objectives
- To investigate the just war theory.
- To explore why the just war theory is important.

Lesson outcomes
By the end of the lesson students should be able to:
- explain why the just war theory is important
- explain their own opinion about the just war theory
- explain why some people may disagree with them.

Prior learning
- Topic 3.1 The United Nations and world peace
- Topic 3.3 Why wars occur

Resources
- Student's Book page 68
- Key Words Sheet 3.2
- Video clip on the effects of bombing

10 mins	**Starter activity**
	1. Put Key Words Sheet 3.2 on students' desks for them to complete as soon as they arrive.
	2. Collect them in for marking.
30 mins	**Main activity**
	1. Show a video on the effects of bombing (examples can be found on the internet).
	2. Discuss whether this bombing could be justified.
	3. Read through the explanation of the just war theory on page 68 of the Student's Book, with plenty of discussion and reference to the key word in the margin.
5 mins	**Plenary activity**
	Set and discuss the homework questions using the exam tip on page 68 of the Student's Book.

Extension
Differentiation by outcome should be possible.

Reinforcement
Less able students should only be set homework question **b**.

Homework
Set questions **b** and **c** from page 68 of the Student's Book:
b Do you think wars can ever be justified? Give two reasons for your point of view.
c Explain what would make a war a just war.

Assessment
- Marking the key words test.
- Answers to the homework questions marked according to the Edexcel mark scheme (Appendix 5).

ICT
The video clip should be shown via the internet and an interactive whiteboard or data projector.

KEY WORDS SHEET 3.2

Draw lines to link the key word with its correct meaning.

Key Word	Meaning
weapons of mass destruction	attacking without being provoked
world peace	intimidating/frightening people weaker than yourself
forgiveness	bringing a fight or struggle to a peaceful conclusion
just war	taking advantage of a weaker group
conflict resolution	the act of stopping blaming someone and/or pardoning them for what they have done wrong
exploitation	a war that is fought for the right reasons and in a right way
the United Nations	the belief that all disputes should be settled by peaceful means
aggression	bringing together people who were opposed to each other
bullying	treating a person or their feelings with consideration
pacifism	an international body set up to promote world peace and co-operation
reconciliation	weapons which can destroy large areas and numbers of people
respect	the ending of war throughout the whole world (the basic aim of the United Nations)

LESSON 7: TOPIC 3.5 DIFFERENCES AMONG CHRISTIANS IN THEIR ATTITUDES TO WAR

Lesson objectives	Lesson outcomes
• To investigate differences among Christians in their attitudes to war. • To explore why there are differences among Christians in their attitudes to war.	By the end of the lesson students should be able to: • explain there are why differences among Christians in their attitudes to war • explain their own opinion about Christian attitudes to war • explain why some people may disagree with them.

Prior learning	Resources
• Topic 3.3 Why wars occur • Topic 3.4 The nature and importance of the theory of just war	• Student's Book pages 69–71 • Starter Sheet 11 • Activity Sheet 5

10 mins	**Starter activity** 1. Put Starter Sheet 11 on students' desks to complete as soon as they sit down. 2. Discuss their answers.
30 mins	**Main activity** 1. Ask students to fill in Activity Sheet 5, in pairs, using pages 69–71 of the Student's Book. 2. If time allows, discuss some of the answers.
5 mins	**Plenary activity** Set and discuss the homework question.

Extension	Reinforcement
Differentiation by outcome should be possible.	Make sure that less able students are given support during the discussions.

Homework	Assessment
Set question **d** from page 71 of the Student's Book: 'Christians should support wars if they are fought for just reasons.' **i** Do you agree? Give reasons for your opinion. **ii** Give reasons why some people may disagree with you. In your answer, you should refer to Christianity.	Answers to the homework question marked according to the Edexcel mark scheme (Appendix 5).
	ICT The video clip should be shown via the internet and an interactive whiteboard or data projector.

STARTER SHEET 11

1. Do you think Jesus would have fought in a war?

2. Give two reasons for your answer.

a

b

ACTIVITY SHEET 5

Using pages 69–71 of the Student's Book fill in the blanks.

Why some Christians are pacifists	
Reason 1	**Reason 2**
Reason 3	**Reason 4**

Why some Christians fight in just wars	
Reason 1	**Reason 2**
Reason 3	**Reason 4**

LESSON 8: TOPIC 3.6 THE ATTITUDES TO WAR OF ONE RELIGION OTHER THAN CHRISTIANITY

Lesson objectives	**Lesson outcomes**
• To investigate the attitudes to war in one religion other than Christianity. • To explore why the followers of one religion other than Christianity have certain attitudes to war.	By the end of the lesson students should be able to: • explain the attitudes to war in one religion other than Christianity • explain their own opinion about the attitudes to war in one religion other than Christianity • explain why some people may disagree with them.

Prior learning	**Resources**
• Topic 3.3 Why wars occur • Topic 3.4 The nature and importance of the theory of just war	Student's Book pages 72, 73, 74–75 or 76

10 mins	**Starter activity** 1. Put this question on the board: 'What do you think is the attitude to war in Islam/Judaism/Hinduism/Sikhism?' 2. As students come in, ask them to write down their answer to the question. 3. Either go round the class asking for their answers and writing them on the board to get a class view or ask students to record their answers on the board.
30 mins	**Main activity** 1. Read through the Student's Book page 72 (Islam), page 73 (Judaism), pages 74–75 (Hinduism) or page 76 (Sikhism), allowing plenty of discussion. 2. Compare their starter answers with what you have read, discussing any similarities or differences.
5 mins	**Plenary activity** Set and explain the homework question using the exam tip on page 72/73/75/76 of the Student's Book.

Extension	**Reinforcement**
Differentiation by outcome should be possible.	• Make sure that less able students are given support in the starter activity. • Advise them that they only need to give one reason for each point of view in the homework.

Homework	**Assessment**
Set question **d** from page 72/73/75/76 of the Student's Book. 'Religious people should never fight in wars.' **i** Do you agree? Give reasons for your opinion. **ii** Give reasons why some people may disagree with you. In your answer, you should refer to at least one religion.	Answers to the homework question marked according to the Edexcel mark scheme (Appendix 5).
	ICT The third part of the starter activity could be done on an interactive whiteboard.

LESSON 9: TOPIC 3.7 CHRISTIAN ATTITUDES TO BULLYING

Lesson objectives	**Lesson outcomes**
• To investigate Christian attitudes to bullying. • To explore why Christians are against bullying.	By the end of the lesson students should be able to: • explain why Christians are against bullying • explain their own opinion about Christian attitudes to bullying • explain why some people may disagree with them.

Prior learning	**Resources**
Topic 3.3 Why wars occur	• Student's Book pages 77–78 • Video clip on bullying

20 mins	**Starter activity**
	 1. Show a short video clip on bullying, for example:
	   • www.bbc.co.uk/videonation/articles/s/suffolk_bullying.shtml is about a schoolboy bullied for how he dresses
	   • www.digizen.org/cyberbullying/fullFilm.aspx is much longer and is produced with actors, but is very good.
	   • See also www.notobullying.org.uk.
	 2. Have a whole-class discussion on how to treat bullying.

20 mins	**Main activity** 1. Ask students to write down, in pairs, one way in which children may be bullied by Christian parents. 2. Select students to feed back their ideas, allowing discussion of each different one. 3. Read through the outline of bullying and the reasons why Christians should be against bullying on pages 77–78 of the Student's Book.
5 mins	**Plenary activity** Set the homework and discuss the exam tip on page 78 of the Student's Book.

Extension	**Reinforcement**
• Differentiation by outcome should be possible. • Students could be given question **d** from page 78 of the Student's Book as an extra homework question.	• Make sure that less able students are paired with a stronger partner. • Ask them to do the first homework question only.

Homework	**Assessment**
Set questions **b** and **c** from page 78 of the Student's Book: **b** Do you think Christians are ever bullies? Give two reasons for your point of view. **c** Explain why Christians are against bullying.	Answers to the homework questions marked according to the Edexcel mark scheme (Appendix 5).
	ICT The starter and main activities could be done using an interactive whiteboard, with student participation.

LESSON 10: TOPIC 3.8 THE ATTITUDES TO BULLYING IN ONE RELIGION OTHER THAN CHRISTIANITY

Lesson objectives	Lesson outcomes
• To investigate the attitudes to bullying in one religion other than Christianity. • To explore why the followers of one religion other than Christianity are against bullying.	By the end of the lesson students should be able to: • explain why the followers of one religion other than Christianity are against bullying • explain their own opinion about attitudes to bullying in one religion other than Christianity • explain why some people may disagree with them.

Prior learning	Resources
Topic 3.7 Christian attitudes to bullying	• Student's Book page 79, 80, 81 or 82 • The school bullying policy

20 mins	**Starter activity** 1. Either give out copies of the school's bullying policy or display it on the interactive whiteboard. 2. Ask the students, in pairs, to identify one way in which the policy could be strengthened. 3. Select students to put their ideas on the board and discuss them as a class. 4. Either print off a copy of the policy and their ideas for each student or ask students to copy down the ideas on their copy of the policy.
20 mins	**Main activity** 1. Ask students to stay in pairs and to use Student's Book page 79 (Islam), page 80 (Judaism), page 81 (Hinduism) or page 82 (Sikhism) to answer question **c**: Choose one religion other than Christianity and explain why its followers are against bullying. 2. Collect in the answers for marking.
5 mins	**Plenary activity** 1. Explain and set the homework question. 2. Inform students that they will have a key words test in the next lesson.

Extension	Reinforcement
Differentiation by outcome should be possible.	Less able students should be paired with a stronger partner for the activities.

Homework	Assessment
• Set question **d** from page 79/80/81/82 of the Student's Book: 'If everyone were religious, there would be no bullies.' i Do you agree? Give reasons for your opinion. ii Give reasons why some people may disagree with you. In your answer, you should refer to at least one religion. • Ask students to revise for a key words test in the next lesson.	Answers to the main activity and homework questions marked according to the Edexcel mark scheme (Appendix 5).
	ICT The starter activity could be done using an interactive whiteboard.

LESSON 11: TOPIC 3.9 RELIGIOUS CONFLICTS WITHIN FAMILIES

Lesson objectives	Lesson outcomes
• To investigate religious conflicts within families. • To explore why there are religious conflicts within families.	By the end of lesson 12 students should be able to: • explain why there are religious conflicts within families • explain their own opinion about religious conflicts within families • explain why some people may disagree with them.

Prior learning	Resources
• Topic 3.7 Christian attitudes to bullying • Topic 3.8 The attitudes to bullying in one religion other than Christianity	• Student's Book pages 83–84 • Key Words Sheet 3.3

15 mins	**Starter activity** 1. Give out Key Words Sheet 3.3 for students to complete individually. 2. Collect them in for marking.
25 mins	**Main activity** Divide the class into groups to prepare one of the following presentations on religious conflict in families, using pages 83–84 of the Student's Book: • Topic 1: Children no longer wanting to take part in their parents' religion • Topic 2: Children wanting to marry a partner from a different faith • Topic 3: Children becoming more religious than their parents • Topic 4: Disagreements over moral issues.
5 mins	**Plenary activity** Check that each group knows who is going to do what to make sure they have their presentations ready for the next lesson.

Extension	Reinforcement
Differentiation by outcome should be possible.	Less able students should be in a group where they will be supported.

Homework	Assessment
Complete the presentations.	Marking the key words test .
	ICT PowerPoint or other software could be used for the presentations.

KEY WORDS SHEET 3.3

Fill in the blanks in the table.

Key Word	Meaning
aggression	
bullying	
conflict resolution	
exploitation	
forgiveness	
just war	
pacifism	
reconciliation	
respect	
the United Nations	
weapons of mass destruction	
world peace	

LESSON 12: TOPIC 3.9 RELIGIOUS CONFLICTS WITHIN FAMILIES

Lesson objectives	Lesson outcomes
• To investigate religious conflicts within families. • To explore why there are religious conflicts within families.	By the end of the lesson students should be able to: • explain why there are religious conflicts within families • explain their own opinion about religious conflicts within families • explain why some people may disagree with them.
Prior learning	**Resources**
• Lesson 11 • Topic 3.7 Christian attitudes to bullying • Topic 3.8 The attitudes to bullying in one religion other than Christianity	• Student's Book pages 83–84 • Student presentations

5 mins	**Starter activity** Students should set up their presentations.
35 mins	**Main activity** 1. Group presentations from lesson 11 on religious conflicts within families, with those students not presenting taking notes. 2. After each presentation students should be given the opportunity to ask the presenters questions, which may lead to some group discussions.
5 mins	**Plenary activity** Set and discuss the homework questions, going through the exam tip on page 84 of the Student's Book.

Extension	Reinforcement
• Differentiation by outcome should be possible. • If time allows, you could follow up these two lessons by watching 'Keeping Mum' or 'East is East' (two films easily available on DVD), discussing the conflicts caused by religion and how the conflicts could have been resolved.	• Make sure that the less able students are given photocopies of a more able student's presentation notes. • Set the first of the homework questions only.

Homework	Assessment

Set questions **c** and **d** from page 84 of the Student's Book:
c Explain why religion can cause conflict within families.
d 'Religion causes more trouble in families than anything else.'
  i Do you agree? Give reasons for your opinion.
  ii Give reasons why some people may disagree with you.
	Answers to the homework questions marked according to the Edexcel mark scheme (Appendix 5).

	ICT PowerPoint or other software could be used for the presentations.

LESSON 13: TOPIC 3.10 CHRISTIAN TEACHINGS ON FORGIVENESS AND RECONCILIATION

Lesson objectives	Lesson outcomes
• To investigate Christian teachings on forgiveness and reconciliation. • To explore why Christians should promote reconciliation.	By the end of the lesson students should be able to: • explain why Christians should promote reconciliation • explain their own opinion about Christian attitudes to forgiveness and reconciliation • explain why some people may disagree with them.
Prior learning • Topic 3.3 Why wars occur • Topic 3.5 Differences among Christians in their attitudes to war • Topic 3.9 Religious conflicts within families	**Resources** • Student's Book page 85 • Selection of newspaper stories

15 mins	**Starter activity** Ask students to read page 85 of the Student's Book.
25 mins	**Main activity** 1. Give out three newspaper articles (for example: one on a young child murdered through abuse or neglect by parents; one on a paedophile case; one on an elderly person beaten up) or display them on the interactive whiteboard from a news website such as www.dailymail.co.uk; www.telegraph.co.uk; www.mirror.co.uk; www.thesun.co.uk; www.the-times.co.uk; www.guardian.co.uk. 2. Ask students to read an article and then discuss whether a Christian should or could forgive the person guilty of the offence, using what they read on page 85 to inform their decision.
5 mins	**Plenary activity** Set the homework questions and discuss the exam tip on page 85 of the Student's Book.

Extension	Reinforcement

• Differentiation by outcome should be possible.
• If you have extra time, you could refer students to:
  ■ the story of Gill Hicks at www.peacedirect.org (Gill Hicks lost her legs in the London bombings and is now working for reconciliation between Christians and Muslims)
  ■ http://famous.y2u.co.uk, where they will find video and print copy about Desmond Tutu's work for reconciliation between blacks and whites in South Africa.
	Advise less able students to do homework question **b** only.

Homework	Assessment

Set questions **b** and **d** from page 85 of the Student's Book:
b Do you think you should always forgive others? Give two reasons for your point of view.
d 'You can't be a good Christian if you do not always forgive others.'
  i Do you agree? Give reasons for your opinion.
  ii Give reasons why some people may disagree with you.
In your answer, you should refer to Christianity.
	Homework questions marked according to the Edexcel mark scheme (Appendix 5).
	
	ICT
	The main activity could involve use of the internet and an interactive whiteboard.

LESSON 14: TOPIC 3.11 THE TEACHINGS ON FORGIVENESS AND RECONCILIATION OF ONE RELIGION OTHER THAN CHRISTIANITY

Lesson objectives	Lesson outcomes
• To investigate teachings on forgiveness and reconciliation in one religion other than Christianity. • To explore why one religion other than Christianity should promote reconciliation.	By the end of the lesson students should be able to: • explain why one religion other than Christianity should promote reconciliation • explain their own opinion about attitudes to forgiveness and reconciliation in one religion other than Christianity • explain why some people may disagree with them.
Prior learning • Topic 3.3 Why wars occur • Topic 3.6 The attitudes to war of one religion other than Christianity • Topic 3.9 Religious conflicts within families	**Resources** • Student's Book page 86, 87, 88 or 89 • Video clip on the Israel/Palestine situation

15 mins	**Starter activity** 1. Show a video clip of the Israel/Palestine situation (for an example see www.paxchristi.org.uk/Wall.html). 2. Have a class discussion on the difficulties of reconciling opposing groups such as Israelis and Palestinians.
25 mins	**Main activity** In pairs, students should use the Student's Book page 86 (Islam), page 87 (Judaism), page 88 (Hinduism) or page 89 (Sikhism) to answer question **c**: Choose one religion other than Christianity and explain why its followers should forgive wrongdoers. Read and discuss the exam tip on page 86 (Islam), page 87, (Judaism), page 88 (Hinduism), page 89 (Sikhism).
5 mins	**Plenary activity** 1. Set and discuss the homework question. 2. Explain that in the next lesson they will be preparing their revision for the end of section test, therefore they must have their complete files with them.

Extension Differentiation by outcome should be possible.	Reinforcement Less able students should be paired with a more able student for the main activity.

Homework Set question **d** from page 86/87/88/89 of the Student's Book: 'You can't be religious if you don't always forgive others.' i Do you agree? Give reasons for your opinion. ii Give reasons why some people may disagree with you. In your answer, you should refer to at least one religion.	Assessment Answers to the main activity and homework questions marked according to the Edexcel mark scheme (Appendix 5).
	ICT For the starter activity you could use the internet and show the video on an interactive whiteboard or via a data projector.

LESSON 15: REVISION OF SECTION 3

Lesson objectives	**Lesson outcomes**
• To ensure that students have all the resources and information they need to revise Section 3. • To explore the assessment methods and objectives used by Edexcel.	By the end of the lesson students should be able to: • revise Section 3 • answer a test paper on Section 3.

Prior learning	**Resources**
Section 3, lessons 1–14	• Student's Book page 90 • Revision Checklist 3 • Edexcel generic mark scheme (Appendix 5, pages 172–73)

20 mins	**Starter activity** 1. Refer back to the students' answers from lesson 1, when they predicted what the most interesting topic in this section would be, and discuss whether their expectations were right or wrong. 2. Give out the revision checklist, which students must fill in using their files.
20 mins	**Main activity** Read through 'How to answer exam questions' on page 90 of the Student's Book, relating each answer to the Edexcel generic mark scheme in Appendix 5, pages 172–73.
5 mins	**Plenary activity** Ensure that everyone is prepared for the test in the next lesson.

Extension Differentiation will be achieved by the outcomes of the test.	**Reinforcement** Make sure that less able students have help in completing the revision checklist.

Homework Revise for the test.	**Assessment** N/A
	ICT N/A

REVISION CHECKLIST 3

Resources required	Tick if I have it
Key Words Sheet 3.1	
Presentation notes on the UN Presentation notes on why wars occur Presentation notes on religious conflicts in families	
Activity Sheet 5	

Homework for Topic 3.1:
b Do you think the United Nations is important? Give two reasons for your point of view.
d 'The United Nations is the best chance for world peace.'
  i Do you agree? Give reasons for your opinion.
  ii Give reasons why some people may disagree with you.	

Homework for Topic 3.2: **b** Do you think religious organisations can stop wars? Give two reasons for your point of view. **c** Explain how religious organisations work for world peace.	
Homework for Topic 3.3: 'Religion is the main cause of wars.' **i** Do you agree? Give reasons for your opinion. **ii** Give reasons why some people may disagree with you.	
Homework for Topic 3.4: **b** Do you think wars can ever be justified? Give two reasons for your point of view. **c** Explain what would make a war a just war.	
Homework for Topic 3.5: 'Christians should support wars if they are fought for just reasons.' **i** Do you agree? Give reasons for your opinion. **ii** Give reasons why some people may disagree with you.	
Homework for Topic 3.6: 'Religious people should never fight in wars.' **i** Do you agree? Give reasons for your opinion. **ii** Give reasons why some people may disagree with you.	
Homework for Topic 3.7: **b** Do you think Christians are ever bullies? Give two reasons for your point of view. **c** Explain why Christians are against bullying.	

Class work and homework for Topic 3.8:
c Choose one religion other than Christianity and explain why its followers are against bullying.
d 'If everyone were religious, there would be no bullies.'
  i Do you agree? Give reasons for your opinion.
  ii Give reasons why some people may disagree with you.	

Homework for Topic 3.9:
c Explain why religion can cause conflict within families.
d 'Religion causes more trouble in families than anything else.'
  i Do you agree? Give reasons for your opinion.
  ii Give reasons why some people may disagree with you.	

Homework for Topic 3.10:
b Do you think you should always forgive others? Give two reasons for your point of view.
d 'You can't be a good Christian if you do not always forgive others.'
  i Do you agree? Give reasons for your opinion.
  ii Give reasons why some people may disagree with you.	

Class work and homework for Topic 3.11:
c Choose one religion other than Christianity and explain why its followers should forgive wrongdoers.
d 'You can't be religious if you don't always forgive others.'
  i Do you agree? Give reasons for your opinion.
  ii Give reasons why some people may disagree with you.	

LESSON 16: SECTION 3 TEST

Lesson objectives To complete the Section 3 Test in 25 minutes under exam conditions.	**Lesson outcome** By the end of the lesson students should be able to assess how well they have understood Section 3.
Prior learning The whole of Section 3	**Resources** • Section 3 Test • Target setting material (Appendix 7, pages 199–201, 204) • Mark scheme (Appendix 6, pages 186–92)

5 mins	**Starter activity** Hand out the Section 3 Test to the students, explaining what is meant by 'under exam conditions'.
30 mins	**Main activity** 1. Ask the students to complete the questions in 25 minutes. 2. Collect the students' answers.
10 mins	**Plenary activity** Explain the target setting process (material for target setting is provided in Appendix 7, pages 199–204)

Extension The test questions allow differentiation by outcome.	**Reinforcement** Make sure that less able students have a reader or computer if they will be allowed these in the exam.
Homework N/A	**Assessment** Answers to the test marked according to the mark scheme (Appendix 6, pages 186–92).
	ICT N/A

SECTION 3 TEST

Section 3 Religion: Peace and conflict

Answer either question 1 or question 2.

1. a) What is conflict resolution? (2 marks)

   b) Do you think you should always forgive others?

     Give two reasons for your point of view. (4 marks)

   c) Explain how religious organisations work for world peace. (8 marks)

   d) 'Religion causes more trouble in families than anything else.'

     (i) Do you agree? Give reasons for your opinion. (3 marks)

     (ii) Give reasons why some people may disagree with you. (3 marks)

   In your answer you should refer to at least one religion.

(Total: 20 marks)

2. a) What is exploitation? (2 marks)

   b) Do you think Christians are ever bullies?

     Give two reasons for your point of view. (4 marks)

   c) Explain why religion can cause conflict within families. (8 marks)

   d) 'Religion is the main cause of wars.'

     (i) Do you agree? Give reasons for your opinion. (3 marks)

     (ii) Give reasons why some people may disagree with you. (3 marks)

   In your answer you should refer to at least one religion.

(Total: 20 marks)

LESSON 1: TOPIC 4.1 THE NEED FOR LAW AND JUSTICE

Lesson objectives	**Lesson outcomes**
• To investigate the need for law and justice. • To explore why society needs law and justice.	By the end of lesson 2 students should be able to: • explain how and why society needs law and justice • explain their own opinion about the need for law and justice • explain why some people may disagree with them.

Prior learning	**Resources**
• Section 1 Religion: Rights and responsibilities • Section 2 Religion: Environmental and medical issues • Section 3 Religion: Peace and conflict	• Student's Book pages 91–93 • Starter Sheet 12

10 mins	**Starter activity** 1. Put Starter Sheet 12 on students' desks for them to complete as soon as they come in. 2. Discuss their answers as a class.
30 mins	**Main activity** 1. Read the introduction to Section 4 on page 91 of the Student's Book and discuss with students why some people might regard this section as the most important section. 2. Divide the class into groups to prepare presentations on the following topics, using pages 92–94 of the Student's Book: • Topic 1: Why we need laws • Topic 2: Why there needs to be a connection between laws and justice.
5 mins	**Plenary activity** Check that each group knows who is going to do what to make sure that they have their presentations ready for the next lesson.

Extension	**Reinforcement**
• Differentiation by outcome should be possible. • Students may wish to do extra research as part of the homework (for example, using the task suggested at www.standards.dfes.gov.uk/schemes2/ks4citizenship/cit04/04q1?view=get).	Less able students should be in a group where they can be supported.

Homework	**Assessment**
Complete the presentations.	N/A
	ICT PowerPoint or other software could be used for the presentations.

STARTER SHEET 12

1. What is law?

2. Write down three laws.

a

b

c

LESSON 2: TOPIC 4.1 THE NEED FOR LAW AND JUSTICE

Lesson objectives	**Lesson outcomes**
• To investigate the need for law and justice. • To explore why society needs law and justice.	By the end of the lesson students should be able to: • explain how and why society needs law and justice • explain their own opinion about the need for law and justice • explain why some people may disagree with them.
Prior learning • Section 4, lesson 1 • Section 1 Religion: Rights and responsibilities • Section 2 Religion: Environmental and medical issues • Section 3 Religion: Peace and conflict	**Resources** • Student's Book pages 92–93 • Student presentations

5 mins	**Starter activity** Students should set up their presentations.
30 mins	**Main activity** 1. Group presentations from lesson 1 on the need for law and justice, with those students not presenting taking notes. 2. After each presentation students should be given the opportunity to ask the presenters questions, which may lead to some group discussions.
5 mins	**Plenary activity** Set and discuss the homework questions using the exam tip on page 93 of the Student's Book.

Extension Differentiation by outcome should be possible.	**Reinforcement** • Make sure that the less able students are given photocopies of a more able student's presentation notes. • Set the first of the homework questions only.
Homework Set questions **b** and **c** from page 93 of the Student's Book: **b** Do you think we need laws? Give two reasons for your point of view. **c** Explain why laws need to be just.	**Assessment** Answers to the homework questions marked according to the Edexcel mark scheme (Appendix 5).
	ICT PowerPoint or other software could be used for the presentations.

LESSON 3: TOPIC 4.2 THEORIES OF PUNISHMENT

Lesson objectives	**Lesson outcomes**
• To investigate theories of punishment. • To explore why there are different theories of punishment.	By the end of the lesson students should be able to: • explain why there are different theories of punishment • explain their own opinion about theories of punishment • explain why some people may disagree with them.
Prior learning Topic 4.1 The need for law and justice	**Resources** • Student's Book pages 94–95 • Starter Sheet 13 • Homework Sheet 3

15 mins	**Starter activity** 1. Put Starter Sheet 13 on students' desks for them to complete as soon as they come in. 2. Select students to come out and write a type of punishment on the board. Leave these on the board.
30 mins	**Main activity** 1. Read through pages 94–95 of the Student's Book, discussing each theory and ensuring that students are aware of the difference between retribution, reform, deterrence and protection. 2. Go to the list of punishments on the board and ask students which theory they belong to – allow discussion of whether a type of punishment can be based on two theories, for example, prison combines protection and reform.
5 mins	**Plenary activity** 1. Set and explain the homework question using the exam tip on page 95 of the Student's Book. 2. Give out and explain the justice questionnaire (Homework Sheet 3). Students should give a copy to at least two Christians, if possible, and should bring the completed questionnaires to the next lesson.

Extension Differentiation by outcome should be possible.	**Reinforcement** Less able students should be paired with a more able partner for the starter activity.
Homework • Set question **b** from page 95 of the Student's Book: What do you think is the best form of punishment? Give two reasons for your point of view. • Homework Sheet 3	**Assessment** Answers to the homework question marked according to the Edexcel mark scheme (Appendix 5).
	ICT The starter activity could be done on an interactive whiteboard.

STARTER SHEET 13

Write down four different types of punishment used in the UK.

1.

2.

3.

4.

HOMEWORK SHEET 3

Christianity and justice questionnaire

As part of my GCSE Religious Studies course, I am studying Christianity and justice. I would be grateful if you could spare a few moments to answer the following questions for me by ticking the appropriate box:

1. Do you go to church?

   At least once a month ☐

   A few times a year ☐

   Just for weddings and funerals ☐

2. Do you think justice is an important issue for Christians?

   Yes ☐

   No ☐

3. Would ideas about justice affect the way you vote in an election?

   Yes ☐

   No ☐

4. Do you do anything to help poor people in the United Kingdom?

   Yes ☐

   No ☐

5. Do you do anything to help poor people in less economically developed countries?

   Yes ☐

   No ☐

LESSON 4: TOPIC 4.3 WHY JUSTICE IS IMPORTANT FOR CHRISTIANS

Lesson objectives • To investigate the Christian attitudes to justice. • To explore why justice is important for Christians.	**Lesson outcomes** By the end of the lesson students should be able to: • explain why justice is important for Christians • explain their own opinion about Christian attitudes to justice • explain why some people may disagree with them.
Prior learning • Topic 4.1 The need for law and justice • Topic 4.2 Theories of punishment	**Resources** • Student's Book pages 96–97 • Starter Sheet 14 • Completed Homework Sheet 3

15 mins	**Starter activity** 1. Display the three parts of Starter Sheet 14 on the board and put a second copy of the tally chart on every desk. 2. As students come in, ask them to fill in the tally chart on their desk from their questionnaires. Students may wish to convert the answers to percentages. To do this they should multiply the total by 100 and divide this by the total number of respondents in the tally chart. For example, if 25 respondents go to church at least once a month and 13 answer that justice is important, then 13 x 100 = 1300 ÷ 25 = 52, so 52% of people going to church once a month think justice is important for Christians. 3. Leave the charts on the board.
25 mins	**Main activity** 1. Read through pages 96–97 of the Student's Book. 2. Discuss the relationship between the importance of justice shown by the tally charts and the importance indicated by the text. 3. Discuss whether justice seems to be more important to Christians who go to church more often.
5 mins	**Plenary activity** Set the homework question and discuss the exam tip on page 97 of the Student's Book, explaining that the questionnaire results could be useful for arguing against.

Extension • Differentiation by outcome should be possible. • The work on converting the tally chart results to percentages could be given to the more able students only.	**Reinforcement** • Make sure that less able students are supported in the discussions. • Advise them that one reason for their own point of view and one for the opposite will be sufficient for the homework.

Homework Set question **d** from page 97 of the Student's Book: 'If everyone was Christian, there would be no injustice.' **i** Do you agree? Give reasons for your opinion. **ii** Give reasons why some people may disagree with you. You should refer to Christianity in your answer.	**Assessment** Answers to the homework question marked according to the Edexcel mark scheme (Appendix 5).
	ICT The starter activity could be done using an interactive whiteboard.

STARTER SHEET 14

Tally charts for results of the Christianity and justice questionnaire

'Once a month' Christians

Question	Yes	No
Do you think justice is an important issue for Christians?		
Would ideas about justice affect the way you vote in an election?		
Do you do anything to help poor people in the United Kingdom?		
Do you do anything to help poor people in less economically developed countries?		

'Few times a year' Christians

Question	Yes	No
Do you think justice is an important issue for Christians?		
Would ideas about justice affect the way you vote in an election?		
Do you do anything to help poor people in the United Kingdom?		
Do you do anything to help poor people in less economically developed countries?		

'Weddings and funerals' Christians

Question	Yes	No
Do you think justice is an important issue for Christians?		
Would ideas about justice affect the way you vote in an election?		
Do you do anything to help poor people in the United Kingdom?		
Do you do anything to help poor people in less economically developed countries?		

Religion and Society Teacher's Resource Pack Third Edition © Hodder Education, 2009

LESSON 5: TOPIC 4.4 WHY JUSTICE IS IMPORTANT FOR THE FOLLOWERS OF ONE RELIGION OTHER THAN CHRISTIANITY

Lesson objectives	Lesson outcomes
• To investigate the attitudes to justice of one religion other than Christianity. • To explore why justice is important in one religion other than Christianity.	By the end of the lesson students should be able to: • explain why justice is important in one religion other than Christianity • explain their own opinion about the attitudes to justice of one religion other than Christianity • explain why some people may disagree with them.

Prior learning	Resources
• Topic 4.1 The need for law and justice • Topic 4.2 Theories of punishment	• Student's Book page 98, 99, 100 or 101 • Key Words Sheet 4.1

10 mins	**Starter activity** Give the students Key Words Sheet 4.1. Ask them to draw a picture or write a word in the prompt column to help them to remember each word.
30 mins	**Main activity** 1. Read through the exam tip in the Student's Book on page 98 (Islam), page 99 (Judaism), page 100 (Hinduism) or page 101 (Sikhism) with the class, discussing as necessary. 2. Ask students to answer question **c** from page 98/99/100/101 of the Student's Book in pairs during the lesson: Choose one religion other than Christianity and explain why justice is important for the followers of that religion. 3. Have a whole-class discussion on whether religious people care more about justice than non-religious people do, putting the main points on the board. These points should be copied down by students or, if using an interactive board, printed off for the students.
5 mins	**Plenary activity** Set the homework question, explaining how the notes from the discussion can be used to help them.

Extension	Reinforcement
Differentiation by outcome should be possible.	Less able students should be paired with a more able partner for the main activity.

Homework	Assessment
Set question **d** from page 98/99/100/101 of the Student's Book: 'Non-religious people don't care as much about justice as religious people do.' **i** Do you agree? Give reasons for your opinion. **ii** Give reasons why some people may disagree with you. In your answer, you should refer to at least one religion.	Answers to the main activity and homework question marked according to the Edexcel mark scheme (Appendix 5).
	ICT Part 3 of the main activity could be done on an interactive whiteboard.

KEY WORDS SHEET 4.1

Key Word	Meaning	Your Prompt
addiction	a recurring compulsion to engage in an activity regardless of its bad effects	
capital punishment	the death penalty for a crime or offence	
crime	an act against the law	
deterrence	the idea that punishments should be of such a nature that they will put people off (deter) committing crimes	
judgement	the act of judging people and their actions	
justice	due allocation of reward and punishment, the maintenance of what is right	
law	rules made by Parliament and enforceable by the courts	
reform	the idea that punishments should try to change criminals so that they will not commit crimes again	
rehabilitation	restore to normal life	
responsibility	being responsible for one's actions	
retribution	the idea that punishments should make criminals pay for what they have done wrong	
sin	an act against the will of God	

Religion and Society Teacher's Resource Pack Third Edition © Hodder Education, 2009

LESSON 6: TOPIC 4.5 THE NATURE OF CAPITAL PUNISHMENT AND NON-RELIGIOUS ARGUMENTS ABOUT CAPITAL PUNISHMENT

Lesson objectives	Lesson outcomes
• To investigate capital punishment. • To explore why there are different non-religious attitudes to capital punishment.	By the end of lesson 7 students should be able to: • explain why there are different non-religious attitudes to capital punishment • explain their own opinion about capital punishment • explain why some people may disagree with them.
Prior learning • Topic 4.2 Theories of punishment • Topic 4.3 Why justice is important for Christians • Topic 4.4 Why justice is important for the followers of one religion other than Christianity	**Resources** • Student's Book pages 102–3 • Video clip of Amnesty International's short animated slide show on capital punishment (www.amnesty.org)

15 mins	**Starter activity** 1. Show the video clip. 2. Discuss the students' reactions to the clip.
25 mins	**Main activity** Divide the class into groups to prepare presentations on the following topics, using pages 102–3 of the Student's Book: • Topic 1: Non-religious arguments against capital punishment • Topic 2: Non-religious arguments in favour of capital punishment.
5 mins	**Plenary activity** Check that each group knows who is going to do what to make sure they have their presentations ready for the next lesson.

Extension	Reinforcement
• Differentiation by outcome should be possible. • Students may wish to do extra research as part of the homework (for example, using www.amnesty.org.uk).	Less able students should be in a group where they will be supported.

Homework	Assessment
Complete the presentations.	N/A
	ICT PowerPoint or other software could be used for the presentations.

LESSON 7: TOPIC 4.5 THE NATURE OF CAPITAL PUNISHMENT AND NON-RELIGIOUS ARGUMENTS ABOUT CAPITAL PUNISHMENT

Lesson objectives • To investigate capital punishment. • To explore why there are different non-religious attitudes to capital punishment.	**Lesson outcomes** By the end of the lesson students should be able to: • explain why there are different non-religious attitudes to capital punishment • explain their own opinion about capital punishment • explain why some people may disagree with them.
Prior learning • Section 4, lesson 6 • Topic 4.2 Theories of punishment • Topic 4.3 Why justice is important for Christians • Topic 4.4 Why justice is important for the followers of one religion other than Christianity	**Resources** • Student's Book pages 102–3 • Student presentations

5 mins	**Starter activity** Students should set up their presentations.
30 mins	**Main activity** 1. Group presentations from lesson 6 on capital punishment, with those students not presenting taking notes. 2. After each presentation students should be given the opportunity to ask the presenters questions, which may lead to some group discussions.
5 mins	**Plenary activity** Set and discuss the homework questions using the exam tip on page 103 of the Student's Book.

Extension Differentiation by outcome should be possible.	**Reinforcement** • Make sure that the less able students are given photocopies of a more able student's presentation notes. • Only set the first of the homework questions for these students.

Homework
• Set questions **b** and **c** from page 103 of the Student's Book:
  b Do you think capital punishment is right? Give two reasons for your point of view.
  c Explain why some non-religious people agree with capital punishment and why some disagree with capital punishment.
• Ask students to revise for a key words test in the next lesson.
	Assessment
	Answers to the homework questions marked according to the Edexcel mark scheme (Appendix 5).

	ICT PowerPoint or other software could be used for the presentations.

LESSON 8: TOPIC 4.6 DIFFERENT ATTITUDES TO CAPITAL PUNISHMENT AMONG CHRISTIANS

Lesson objectives • To investigate different Christian attitudes to capital punishment. • To explore why there are different Christian attitudes to capital punishment.	**Lesson outcomes** By the end of the lesson students should be able to: • explain why Christians have different attitudes to capital punishment • explain their own opinion about Christian attitudes to capital punishment • explain why some people may disagree with them.
Prior learning • Topic 4.3 Why justice is important for Christians • Topic 4.5 The nature of capital punishment and non-religious arguments about capital punishment	**Resources** • Student's Book pages 104–5 • Key Words Sheet 4.2

10 mins	**Starter activity** 1. Give out Key Words Sheet 4.2 for students to complete individually. 2. Collect them in for marking.
30 mins	**Main activity** 1. Ask students to decide, in pairs, what they think the Christian attitude to capital punishment is. 2. Ask for student feedback and write a selection of their answers on the board. 3. Read through pages 104–5 from the Student's Book, discussing any differences with the answers on the board.
5 mins	**Plenary activity** Set and explain the homework question using the exam tip on page 105 of the Student's Book and referring back to the class discussions.

Extension Differentiation by outcome should be possible.	**Reinforcement** Advise less able students that one reason for their own point of view and one for the opposite will be sufficient for the homework question.
Homework Set question **d** from page 105 of the Student's Book: 'You can't be a good Christian and support capital punishment.' i Do you agree? Give reasons for your opinion. ii Give reasons why some people may disagree with you. In your answer, you should refer to Christianity.	**Assessment** • Marking the key words test • Answers to the homework question marked according to the Edexcel mark scheme (Appendix 5).
	ICT The feedback in the main activity could be done on an interactive whiteboard.

KEY WORDS SHEET 4.2

Fill in the blanks in the table.

Key Word	Meaning
addiction	
capital punishment	
	an act against the law
	the idea that punishments should be of such a nature that they will put people off (deter) committing crimes
judgement	
justice	
	rules made by Parliament and enforceable by the courts
	the idea that punishments should try to change criminals so that they will not commit crimes again
rehabilitation	
responsibility	
	the idea that punishments should make criminals pay for what they have done wrong
	an act against the will of God

Religion and Society Teacher's Resource Pack Third Edition © Hodder Education, 2009

LESSON 9: TOPIC 4.7 DIFFERENT ATTITUDES TO CAPITAL PUNISHMENT IN ONE RELIGION OTHER THAN CHRISTIANITY

Lesson objectives	Lesson outcomes
• To investigate the attitudes to capital punishment in one religion other than Christianity. • To explore why there are different attitudes to capital punishment in one religion other than Christianity.	By the end of the lesson students should be able to: • explain why there are different attitudes to capital punishment in one religion other than Christianity • explain their own opinion about the attitudes to capital punishment in one religion other than Christianity • explain why some people may disagree with them.
Prior learning	**Resources**
• Topic 4.4 Why justice is important for the followers of one religion other than Christianity • Topic 4.5 The nature of capital punishment and non-religious arguments about capital punishment	• Student's Book page 106, 107, 108 or 109 • Starter Sheet 15

15 mins	**Starter activity** 1. Put a copy of Starter Sheet 15 on the desks before students arrive. 2. Ask the students to read the article and decide whether Nur-Pashi Kulayev should be executed. 3. Take a vote and then discuss the results.

25 mins	**Main activity**
	1. Display question **d** on the board: 'You can't be religious and support capital punishment.'
	   i Do you agree? Give reasons for your opinion.
	   ii Give reasons why some people may disagree with you.
	   In your answer, you should refer to either Islam, Judaism, Hinduism or Sikhism.
	2. Explain the question and how best to answer it.
	3. Students should work in pairs to answer the question, using the Student's Book page 106 (Islam), 107 (Judaism), 108 (Hinduism) or 109 (Sikhism).
	4. Collect the answers in for marking.

5 mins	**Plenary activity** Set and explain the homework and discuss the exam tip on page 106/107/108/109 of the Student's Book.

Extension	Reinforcement
• Differentiation by outcome should be possible. • Students could do research on executions in religious countries using the BBC News website http://news.bbc.co.uk.	• Less able students should be paired with a more able partner for the main activity. • Only set the first homework question for these students.

Homework	Assessment
Set questions **b** and **c** from page 106/107/108/109 of the Student's Book: **b** Do you think religious people should support capital punishment? Give two reasons for your point of view. **c** Choose one religion other than Christianity and explain why some of its followers support capital punishment.	Answers to the main activity and homework questions marked according to the Edexcel mark scheme (Appendix 5).
	ICT The first parts of the main activity could be done on an interactive whiteboard.

STARTER SHEET 15

Prosecutor calls for death penalty in Beslan trial

Published date: 10 February 2006
By: Fatima Tlisova
In: Nalchik, Russia

A prosecutor has demanded the death penalty for the man alleged to be the sole surviving attacker in the Beslan school siege.

Nur-Pashi Kulayev is on trial in southern Russia for his alleged role in the attack by 32 terrorists which left more than 330 people dead, nearly half of them children. A verdict could be delivered by the end of the month, a prosecutor's spokesman said.

With the trial in its ninth month, Nikolai Shepel told the court that Kulayev should be executed, something many survivors and relatives of victims have called for. Kulayev, who faces terrorism, murder and other charges, has reportedly confessed to taking part in the raid but insisted he killed nobody.

'Based on the sum of the charges presented, I request that you pass a sentence of capital punishment,' Mr Shepel said in televised comments that were met with applause by observers in the courtroom.

Despite Mr Shepel's request, it was unclear whether Kulayev could be executed since Russia imposed a moratorium [suspension of an activity] on the death penalty in 1996 when it joined the Council of Europe.

Many Russians support capital punishment, and some government officials have proposed lifting the moratorium for convicted terrorists.

(Source: http://news.scotsman.com/beslanschoolsiege/Prosecutor-calls-for-death-penalty.2749673.jp)

LESSON 10: TOPIC 4.8 THE LAWS ON DRUGS AND ALCOHOL

Lesson objectives	**Lesson outcomes**
• To investigate the UK laws on drugs and alcohol. • To explore why there are laws on drugs and alcohol.	By the end of the lesson students should be able to: • explain why there are laws on drugs and alcohol • explain their own opinion about the UK laws on drugs and alcohol • explain why some people may disagree with them.
Prior learning Topic 4.1 The need for law and justice	**Resources** • Student's Book pages 110–11 • Starter Sheet 16

10 mins	**Starter activity** 1. Put Starter Sheet 16 on students' desks for them to complete as soon as they come in. 2. Display the correct answers on the board, with discussion of any differences between student responses and the correct answers (these are in the Student's Book, page 111). 3. Students should amend their answers where necessary.
30 mins	**Main activity** 1. Read the information on the UK laws on tobacco on page 110 of the Student's Book. Students should make a note of three laws on the back of Starter Sheet 16. 2. Read through the UK laws on alcohol on page 110. Students should make a note of three laws on the back of Starter Sheet 16. 3. Read through the UK laws on illegal drugs on page 111, allowing plenty of discussion.
5 mins	**Plenary activity** Set and explain the homework, using the exam tip on page 111 of the Student's Book.

Extension Differentiation by outcome should be possible.	**Reinforcement** Less able students could be paired with a more able partner for the starter activity.
Homework Set question **b** from page 111 of the Student's Book: Do you think the laws on drugs and alcohol are fair? Give two reasons for your point of view.	**Assessment** Answers to the homework question marked according to the Edexcel mark scheme (Appendix 5).
	ICT The feedback on the starter activity could be presented and analysed on an interactive whiteboard.

STARTER SHEET 16

Put each of the drugs into the appropriate column: class A, class B or class C drugs.

Possession of Class A (up to 7 years in prison)	Possession of Class B (up to 5 years in prison)	Possession of Class C (up to 2 years in prison)

COCAINE

METHYLPHENIDATE (Ritalin)

PAINKILLERS

HEROIN

AMPHETAMINES (injection)

CRACK

ECSTACY

LSD

CANNABIS

MAGIC MUSHROOMS

TRANQUILLISERS

AMPHETAMINES

LESSON 11: TOPIC 4.9 SOCIAL AND HEALTH PROBLEMS CAUSED BY DRUGS AND ALCOHOL

Lesson objectives	Lesson outcomes
• To investigate social and health problems caused by drugs and alcohol. • To explore how and why drugs and alcohol cause social and health problems.	By the end of lesson 12 students should be able to: • explain how and why drugs and alcohol cause social and health problems • explain why some people may disagree with them.

Prior learning	Resources
Topic 4.8 The laws on drugs and alcohol	• Student's Book pages 112–13 • Starter Sheet 17

10 mins	**Starter activity** 1. Put Starter Sheet 17 on students' desks to complete as soon as they sit down. 2. When they are completed, a selection of student answers should be displayed on the board and discussed.
30 mins	**Main activity** 1. Explain to the students what is meant by a led discussion: you have some people in a group who have discovered some expert information about a topic and they then begin a discussion on the topic, feeding in their information, but allowing the people without the expert information to feed in their opinions. 2. Divide the class into three sets of groups to prepare to lead discussions, using pages 112–13 of the Student's Book, on the following topics: • Group 1: Social and health problems of tobacco • Group 2: Social and health problems of alcohol • Group 3: Social and health problems of drugs.
5 mins	**Plenary activity** Make sure the students are prepared to lead discussions in the next lesson.

Extension	Reinforcement
Differentiation by outcome should be possible.	Less able students should be put in a group where they can receive support.

Homework	Assessment
Complete the preparation for leading discussions in the next lesson.	N/A
	ICT • The starter activity could be done by putting the answers on an interactive whiteboard. • The led discussions could begin with a PowerPoint presentation.

STARTER SHEET 17

Look at the photo below.

Answer these questions:

1. What are the potential dangers facing the drunken girl?

2. What is binge drinking?

LESSON 12: TOPIC 4.9 SOCIAL AND HEALTH PROBLEMS CAUSED BY DRUGS AND ALCOHOL

Lesson objectives	**Lesson outcomes**
• To investigate social and health problems caused by drugs and alcohol. • To explore how and why drugs and alcohol cause social and health problems.	By the end of the lesson students should be able to: • explain how and why drugs and alcohol cause social and health problems • explain why some people may disagree with them.

Prior learning	**Resources**
• Section 4, lesson 11 • Topic 4.8 The laws on drugs and alcohol	Student's Book pages 112–13

5 mins	**Starter activity** Make sure students are ready to make notes on the discussions.
30 mins	**Main activity** 1. Student led discussion on social and health problems of tobacco, with students making notes. 2. Student led discussion on social and health problems of alcohol, with students making notes. 3. Student led discussion on social and health problems of drugs, with students making notes.
10 mins	**Plenary activity** Set the homework and discuss the exam tip on page 113, ensuring that students understand the questions.

Extension	**Reinforcement**
Differentiation by outcome should be possible.	• Less able students should be put in a group where they can receive support and should be given a photocopy of a more able student's notes on the discussions. • Advise these students that they only need to answer the second homework question.

Homework	**Assessment**

Set questions **c** and **d** from page 113 of the Student's Book:
 c Explain why some people think alcohol is the worst drug.
 d 'Using drugs doesn't harm anyone.'
  i Do you agree? Give reasons for your opinion.
  ii Give reasons why some people may disagree with you.
	Answers to the homework questions marked according to the Edexcel mark scheme (Appendix 5).

	ICT The lead in to the discussions could be done using PowerPoint or similar software.

LESSON 13: TOPIC 4.10 DIFFERENT ATTITUDES TO DRUGS AND ALCOHOL IN CHRISTIANITY

Lesson objectives	Lesson outcomes
• To investigate Christian attitudes to drugs and alcohol. • To explore why there are different attitudes to drugs and alcohol in Christianity.	By the end of the lesson students should be able to: • explain why there are different Christian attitudes to drugs and alcohol • explain their own opinion about Christian attitudes to drugs and alcohol • explain why some people may disagree with them.

Prior learning	Resources
• Topic 4.8 The laws on drugs and alcohol • Topic 4.9 Social and health problems caused by drugs and alcohol	• Student's Book pages 114–15 • Starter Sheet 18 • Fact Sheet 4

15 mins	**Starter activity** 1. Put Starter Sheet 18 on the desks for students to complete as soon as they arrive. 2. Give out Fact Sheet 4. Ask the students to read it and amend their starter answers if necessary. 3. Discuss whether they were surprised at any differences.
25 mins	**Main activity** 1. Read through pages 114–15 of the Student's Book. 2. Have a class discussion about which attitude they think is the most Christian.
5 mins	**Plenary activity** Set the homework and discuss the exam tip on page 115 of the Student's Book.

Extension	Reinforcement
• Differentiation by outcome should be possible. • Students could be set question **d** from page 115 as an extra homework question: 'You can still be a good Christian and drink alcohol.' i Do you agree? Give reasons for your opinion. ii Give reasons why some people may disagree with you. In your answer you should refer to Christianity.	Less able students may need to be paired with a more able partner for the starter activity.

Homework	Assessment
• Set question **c** from page 115 of the Student's Book: Explain why some Christians drink alcohol, but others do not. • Ask students to revise for a key words test in the next lesson.	Answers to the homework question marked according to the Edexcel mark scheme (Appendix 5).
	ICT The discussions in the starter and main activity could be recorded and analysed using an interactive whiteboard.

STARTER SHEET 18

Write in the Units column how many units of alcohol you think each drink contains.

Drink	Units
standard pub measure of spirits (35ml)	
2 pints of beer or lager	
2 small glasses of wine	
70cl 5% abv	

? ?

FACT SHEET 4

What are the recommended limits for alcohol?

- **Men** should drink no more than 21 units of alcohol per week (and no more than four units in any one day).
- **Women** should drink no more than 14 units of alcohol per week (and no more than three units in any one day).

What is a unit of alcohol?

One unit of alcohol is about equal to:

- half a pint of ordinary strength beer, lager or cider

- a small pub measure (25ml) of spirits.

There are one and a half units of alcohol in:

- a small glass (125ml) of ordinary strength wine

- a standard pub measure (35ml) of spirits.

A more accurate way of calculating units is to use the percentage value of alcohol in a drink. The percentage alcohol by volume (% abv) of a drink equals the number of units in one litre of that drink. For example:

- Strong beer at 6% abv has six units in one litre. If you drink half a litre (500ml) – just under a pint – then you have had three units.

- Wine at 14% abv has 14 units in one litre. If you drink a quarter of a litre (250ml) – two small glasses – then you have had three and a half units.

Some other examples

Three pints of beer, three times per week, is *at least* 18–20 units per week. That is nearly the upper weekly safe limit for a man. However, each drinking session of three pints is *at least* six units, which is more than the safe limit advised for any one day. Another example: a 750ml bottle of 12% wine contains nine units. If you drink two bottles of 12% wine over a week, that is 18 units. This is above the upper safe limit for a woman.

(Source: adapted from www.patient.co.uk/showdoc/23069189/)

? ?

LESSON 14: TOPIC 4.11 ATTITUDES TO DRUGS AND ALCOHOL IN ONE RELIGION OTHER THAN CHRISTIANITY

Lesson objectives	**Lesson outcomes**
• To investigate attitudes to drugs and alcohol in one religion other than Christianity. • To explore whether and why there are different attitudes to drugs and alcohol in that religion.	By the end of the lesson students should be able to: • explain the attitudes to drugs and alcohol in one religion other than Christianity • explain their own opinion about the attitudes to drugs and alcohol in one religion other than Christianity • explain why some people may disagree with them.

Prior learning	**Resources**
• Topic 4.8 The laws on drugs and alcohol • Topic 4.9 Social and health problems caused by drugs and alcohol	• Student's Book page 116, 117, 118 or 119 • Key Words Sheet 4.3 • Activity Sheet 6

10 mins	**Starter activity** 1. Give out Key Words Sheet 4.3 for students to complete individually. 2. Collect them in for marking.
30 mins	**Main activity** 1. Give every student a copy of Activity Sheet 6. 2. Read through the Student's Book page 116 (Islam), page 117 (Judaism), page 118 (Hinduism) or page 119 (Sikhism). As you read, students should complete the Activity Sheet. 3. Discuss students' own opinions about the statement on the Activity Sheet.
5 mins	**Plenary activity** 1. Set the homework question and discuss the exam tip on page 116/117/118/119 of the Student's Book. 2. Explain that in the next lesson they will be preparing their revision for the end of section test, therefore they must have their complete files with them.

Extension Differentiation by outcome should be possible.	**Reinforcement** Less able students should be given a photocopy of a more able student's Activity Sheet.
Homework Set question **c** from page 116/117/118/119 of the Student's Book: Explain the attitudes to alcohol consumption in one religion other than Christianity.	**Assessment** • Marking the key words test. • Answers to the homework question marked according to the Edexcel mark scheme (Appendix 5).
	ICT N/A

KEY WORDS SHEET 4.3

Fill in the blanks in the table.

Key Word	Meaning
addiction	
capital punishment	
crime	
deterrence	
judgement	
justice	
law	
reform	
rehabilitation	
responsibility	
retribution	
sin	

ACTIVITY SHEET 6

'You can't be religious and sell alcohol and tobacco.'

For	Against

'You can't be religious and sell alcohol and tobacco.'

LESSON 15: REVISION OF SECTION 4

Lesson objectives	Lesson outcomes
• To ensure that students have all the resources and information they need to revise Section 4. • To explore the assessment methods and objectives used by Edexcel.	By the end of the lesson students should be able to: • revise Section 4 • answer a test paper on Section 4.

Prior learning	Resources
Section 4, lessons 1–14	• Student's Book page 120 • Revision Checklist 4 • Edexcel generic mark scheme (Appendix 5, pages 172–73)

20 mins	**Starter activity** Give out the revision checklist, which students must fill in using their files.
20 mins	**Main activity** Read through 'How to answer exam questions' on page 120 of the Student's Book, relating each answer to the Edexcel generic mark scheme in Appendix 5, pages 172–73.
5 mins	**Plenary activity** Ensure that everyone is prepared for the test in the next lesson.

Extension	Reinforcement
Differentiation will be achieved by the outcomes of the test.	Make sure that less able students have help in completing the revision checklist.

Homework	Assessment
Revise for the test.	N/A
	ICT N/A

REVISION CHECKLIST 4

Resources required	Tick if I have it
Key Words Sheet 4.1	
Presentation notes on the need for law and justice Presentation notes on capital punishment Presentation notes on social and health problems of tobacco, drugs and alcohol	
Tally charts for results of the Christianity and justice questionnaire	
Results of discussions on religious people and justice	
Starter Sheet 16	
Activity Sheet 6	
Fact Sheet 4	
Homework for Topic 4.1: b Do you think we need laws? Give two reasons for your point of view. c Explain why laws need to be just.	
Homework for Topic 4.2: What do you think is the best form of punishment? Give two reasons for your point of view.	
Homework for Topic 4.3: 'If everyone was Christian, there would be no injustice.' i Do you agree? Give reasons for your opinion. ii Give reasons why some people may disagree with you.	

Class work and homework for Topic 4.4:
c Choose one religion other than Christianity and explain why justice is important for the followers of that religion
d 'Non-religious people don't care as much about justice as religious people do.'
  i Do you agree? Give reasons for your opinion.
  ii Give reasons why some people may disagree with you.	

Homework for Topic 4.5: b Do you think capital punishment is right? Give two reasons for your point of view. c Explain why some non-religious people agree with capital punishment and why some disagree with capital punishment.	
Homework for Topic 4.6: 'You can't be a good Christian and support capital punishment.' i Do you agree? Give reasons for your opinion. ii Give reasons why some people may disagree with you.	

Class work and homework for Topic 4.7:
d 'You can't be religious and support capital punishment.'
  i Do you agree? Give reasons for your opinion.
  ii Give reasons why some people may disagree with you.
b Do you think religious people should support capital punishment? Give two reasons for your point of view.
c Choose one religion other than Christianity and explain why some of its followers support capital punishment.	

Homework for Topic 4.8: Do you think the laws on drugs and alcohol are fair? Give two reason for your point of view.	

Homework for Topic 4.9:
c Explain why some people think alcohol is the worst drug.
d 'Using drugs doesn't harm anyone.'
  i Do you agree? Give reasons for your opinion.
  ii Give reasons why some people may disagree with you.	

Homework for Topic 4.10: Explain why some Christians drink alcohol, but others do not.	
Homework for Topic 4.11: Explain the attitudes to alcohol consumption in one religion other than Christianity.	

LESSON 16: SECTION 4 TEST

Lesson objectives To complete the Section 4 Test in 25 minutes under exam conditions.	**Lesson outcomes** By the end of the lesson students should be able to assess how well they have understood Section 4.
Prior learning The whole of Section 4	**Resources** • Section 4 Test • Target setting material (Appendix 7, pages 199–201, 205) • Mark scheme (Appendix 6, pages 193–98)

5 mins	**Starter activity** Hand out the Section 4 Test to the students, explaining what is meant by 'under exam conditions'.
30 mins	**Main activity** 1. Ask the students to complete the questions in 25 minutes. 2. Collect the students' answers.
10 mins	**Plenary activity** Explain the target setting process (material for target setting is provided in Appendix 7, pages 199–205)

Extension The test questions allow differentiation by outcome.	**Reinforcement** Make sure that less able students have a reader or computer if they will be allowed these in the exam.
Homework N/A	**Assessment** Answers to the test marked according to the mark scheme (Appendix 6, pages 193–98).
	ICT N/A

SECTION 4 TEST

Section 4: Religion: Crime and punishment

Answer either question 1 or question 2.

1. a) What is addiction? (2 marks)

b) Do you think religious people should support capital punishment?

Give two reasons for your point of view. (4 marks)

c) Explain the attitudes to alcohol consumption in one religion other than Christianity. (8 marks)

d) 'Non-religious people don't care as much about justice as religious people do.'

(i) Do you agree? Give reasons for your opinion. (3 marks)

(ii) Give reasons why some people may disagree with you. (3 marks)

In your answer you should refer to at least one religion.

(Total: 20 marks)

2. a) What is rehabilitation? (2 marks)

b) Do you think we need laws?

Give two reasons for your point of view. (4 marks)

c) Choose one religion other than Christianity and explain why some of its followers support capital punishment. (8 marks)

d) 'Using drugs doesn't harm anyone.'

(i) Do you agree? Give reasons for your opinion. (3 marks)

(ii) Give reasons why some people may disagree with you. (3 marks)

In your answer you should refer to at least one religion.

(Total: 20 marks)

APPENDIX 1

GENERIC LESSON PLAN AND WORKSHEETS FOR SECTION 1

Worksheets are provided for all the lessons in Section 1 (pages 1–35) along with a lesson plan (below) where most of the boxes have been left blank to enable you to adapt it for use with any of the worksheets.

LESSON PLAN

Lesson title
•

| **Lesson objectives** | **Lesson outcomes** |
| • | • |

Prior learning	**Resources**
•	• Student's Book pages xx–xx
	• Worksheet xx

5 mins	**Starter activity** Give out the worksheets and Student's Books, ensuring that everyone knows what they have to do.
25 mins	**Main activity** Ask students to complete Worksheet xx in pairs using the Student's Book pages xx–xx.
15 mins	**Plenary activity** Have a feedback session, going over the answers and ensuring that all students have amended their answers where necessary.

Extension Differentiation by outcome should be possible.	**Reinforcement** • Less able students should be paired with more able ones.

| **Homework** • | **Assessment** • |
| | **ICT** • |

WORKSHEET 1.1: THE BIBLE AS A BASIS FOR MAKING MORAL DECISIONS

Use pages 2–3 of the Student's Book to answer these questions:

1. What is a moral decision?

2. Give four reasons why some Christians use only the Bible as a guide for making moral decisions.

3. Why do some Christians think the Bible does not have complete authority?

4. Do you think Christians should use only the Bible for making moral decisions? Give two reasons for your point of view.

5. Explain why some people may disagree with you.

WORKSHEET 1.2: THE AUTHORITY OF THE CHURCH AS A BASIS FOR MAKING MORAL DECISIONS

Use pages 4–5 of the Student's Book to answer these questions:

1. **What is the difference between church and Church?**

2. **What do many Christians believe the Church has the right to say about the Bible?**

3. **Give five reasons why some Christians use only the teachings of the Church for making moral decisions.**

4. **Do you think Christians should use only the teachings of the Church for making moral decisions? Give two reasons for your point of view.**

5. **Explain why some people may disagree with you.**

WORKSHEET 1.3: THE ROLE OF CONSCIENCE AS A GUIDE IN MAKING MORAL DECISIONS

Use pages 6–7 of the Student's Book to answer these questions:

1. **What is conscience?**

2. **Give four reasons why some Christians believe they should follow their conscience when making moral decisions.**

3. **Give three reasons why some Christians do not always follow their conscience.**

4. **Do you think Christians should always follow their conscience? Give two reasons for your point of view.**

Religion and Society Teacher's Resource Pack Third Edition © Hodder Education, 2009

WORKSHEET 1.4: SITUATION ETHICS AS A GUIDE FOR MAKING MORAL DECISIONS

Use pages 8–9 of the Student's Book to answer these questions:

1. What is situation ethics?

2. Why do some Christians think they should use only situation ethics when making a moral decision?

3. Why do some Christians disagree with situation ethics?

4. Do you think situation ethics is a good way of making moral decisions? Give two reasons for your point of view.

WORKSHEET 1.5: WHY SOME CHRISTIANS USE A VARIETY OF AUTHORITIES IN MAKING MORAL DECISIONS

Use pages 10–11 of the Student's Book to answer these questions:

1. Why may Protestants who usually use the Bible have to use a different source of authority?

2. Why may Catholics sometimes feel they have to use different guidance from the Magisterium?

3. Why may a Christian who usually uses their conscience sometimes need another guide?

4. Explain why Christians who usually use situation ethics may need other guidance.

5. Do you think any Christian follows all the Bible teachings in Leviticus? Give two reasons.

WORKSHEET 1.6: HUMAN RIGHTS IN THE UNITED KINGDOM

Use pages 12–13 of the Student's Book to answer these questions:

1. What are human rights?

2. What gave UK citizens their human rights?

3. Write down what you consider to be the five most important human rights.

4. Do you think it is important for us to have laws protecting our human rights? Give two reasons for your point of view.

5. Explain why some people may disagree with you.

WORKSHEET 1.7: WHY HUMAN RIGHTS ARE IMPORTANT FOR CHRISTIANS

Use pages 14–15 of the Student's Book to answer these questions:

1. Why are human rights important for Christians?

2. Why may some human rights cause problems for Christians?

3. Look at the first passage in the margin and explain how it shows the importance of human rights.

4. Look at the second passage in the margin and explain how it shows the problems of human rights.

5. Do you think human rights are important for Christians? Give two reasons for your point of view.

6. Explain why some people may disagree with you.

WORKSHEET 1.8: WHY IT IS IMPORTANT TO TAKE PART IN DEMOCRATIC AND ELECTORAL PROCESSES

Use pages 16–17 of the Student's Book to answer these questions:

1. What are democratic and electoral processes?

2. Give four reasons why people should take part in democratic and electoral processes.

3. Why is it important to be able to vote for or against the people who set tax rates?

4. Do you think it is important to vote in elections? Give two reasons for your point of view.

5. Explain why some people may disagree with you.

WORKSHEET 1.9: CHRISTIAN TEACHINGS ON MORAL DUTIES AND RESPONSIBILITIES

Use pages 18–19 of the Student's Book to answer these questions:

1. What is social change?

2. Why may the Golden Rule encourage Christians to work for social change?

3. Why may the Parable of the Sheep and the Goats encourage Christians to work for social change?

4. Why may 'Am I my brother's keeper?' encourage Christians to work for social change?

5. Do you think Christians should always treat others as they want to be treated? Give two reasons for your point of view.

6. Explain why some people may disagree with you.

WORKSHEET 1.10: THE NATURE OF GENETIC ENGINEERING, INCLUDING CLONING

Use pages 20–21 of the Student's Book to answer these questions:

1. What is genetic engineering?

2. What is genetic research based on?

3. Give three reasons in favour of genetic engineering.

4. Give three reasons against genetic engineering.

5. Do you think genetic engineering should be allowed? Give two reasons for your point of view.

WORKSHEET 1.11: DIFFERENT ATTITUDES TO GENETIC ENGINEERING AND CLONING IN CHRISTIANITY

Use pages 22–23 of the Student's Book to answer these questions:

1. Why do some Christians agree with genetic engineering?

2. Why do some people disagree with the cloning part of genetic research?

3. Why are some Christians against any form of genetic engineering?

4. Which Christian view of genetic engineering do you agree with? Give two reasons for your point of view.

APPENDIX 2

GENERIC LESSON PLAN AND WORKSHEETS FOR SECTION 2

Worksheets are provided for all the lessons in Section 2 (pages 36–65) along with a lesson plan (below) where most of the boxes have been left blank to enable you to adapt it for use with any of the worksheets.

LESSON PLAN

Lesson title
•

Lesson objectives	**Lesson outcomes**
•	•

Prior learning	**Resources**
•	• Student's Book pages xx–xx
	• Worksheet xx

5 mins	**Starter activity** Give out the worksheets and Student's Books, ensuring that everyone knows what they have to do.
25 mins	**Main activity** Ask students to complete Worksheet xx in pairs using the Student's Book pages xx–xx.
15 mins	**Plenary activity** Have a feedback session, going over the answers and ensuring that all students have amended their answers where necessary.

Extension Differentiation by outcome should be possible.	**Reinforcement** • Less able students should be paired with more able ones.

Homework •	**Assessment** •
	ICT •

WORKSHEET 2.1: GLOBAL WARMING

Use pages 26–28 of the Student's Book to answer these questions:

1. What is global warming?

2. How may the greenhouse effect cause global warming?

3. How may natural climate change cause global warming?

4. How may solar activity cause global warming?

5. How could the problem of global warming be solved?

6. Do you think global warming is a problem? Give at least two reasons for your point of view.

WORKSHEET 2.2: FORMS OF POLLUTION AND THEIR POSSIBLE SOLUTIONS

Use pages 29–31 of the Student's Book to answer these questions:

1. Why is acid rain a problem, and how could it be solved?

2. Why is human waste a problem, and how could it be solved?

3. Why is eutrophication a problem, and how could it be solved?

4. Why is nuclear waste a problem, and how could it be solved?

5. Do you think the problems of pollution can be solved? Give two reasons for your point of view.

7. Explain why some people may disagree with you.

WORKSHEET 2.3: THE SCARCITY OF NATURAL RESOURCES

Use pages 32–33 of the Student's Book to answer these questions:

1. What is the difference between renewable resources and finite resources?

2. What are the problems with finite resources?

3. Do you think we can solve the problem of resources? Give at least three reasons.

4. Explain why some people may disagree with you.

WORKSHEET 2.4: CHRISTIAN TEACHINGS ON STEWARDSHIP

Use pages 34–35 of the Student's Book to answer these questions:

1. What is stewardship?

2. What does the Bible teach about stewardship?

3. How do Christian beliefs about stewardship affect their attitudes to the environment?

4. Do you think Christians care more about the environment than non-Christians? Give at least two reasons.

5. Explain why some people may disagree with you.

WORKSHEET 2.5: THE TEACHINGS OF ONE RELIGION OTHER THAN CHRISTIANITY ON STEWARDSHIP

Use the Student's Book pages 36–37 (Islam), pages 38–39 (Judaism), pages 40–41 (Hinduism) or pages 42–43 (Sikhism) to answer these questions:

1. What does Islam/Judaism/Hinduism/Sikhism teach about stewardship?

2. How do these beliefs affect the attitudes to the environment of Muslims/Jews/Hindus/Sikhs?

3. Do you think religion is more likely to solve environmental problems than governments? Give at least three reasons.

4. Explain why some people may disagree with you.

WORKSHEET 2.6: THE NATURE AND IMPORTANCE OF MEDICAL TREATMENTS FOR INFERTILITY

Use pages 44–45 of the Student's Book to answer these questions:

1. What are the main treatments for infertility?

2. What is the Human Fertilisation and Embryology Authority?

3. Why are infertility treatments important?

4. Do you think everyone has a right to free infertility treatments? Give two reasons for your point of view.

5. Explain why some people may disagree with you.

WORKSHEET 2.7: DIFFERENT ATTITUDES TO INFERTILITY TREATMENTS AMONG CHRISTIANS

Use pages 46–47 of the Student's Book to answer these questions:

1. What is the Catholic attitude to medical treatments for infertility?

2. What do you think are the main reasons for Catholics having this attitude?

3. What is the attitude to medical treatments for infertility of other Christians?

4. What do you think are the main reasons for non-Catholic Christians having this attitude?

5. Do you think Christians should be allowed to use any form of infertility treatments they wish? Give your reasons.

WORKSHEET 2.8: ATTITUDES TO INFERTILITY TREATMENTS IN ONE RELIGION OTHER THAN CHRISTIANITY

Use the Student's Book page 48 (Islam), page 49 (Judaism), page 50 (Hinduism) or page 51 (Sikhism) to answer these questions:

1. **Which medical treatments for infertility are accepted by most/many Muslims/Jews/Hindus/Sikhs?**

2. **What are the reasons for these treatments being accepted?**

3. **Why do Muslims/Jews/Hindus/Sikhs reject other treatments?**

4. **Why do some Muslims/Jews/Hindus/Sikhs accept some other treatments?**

5. **Do you think religion should tell people which medical treatments they can use and which they can't use? Give at least two reasons.**

6. **Explain why some people may disagree with you.**

WORKSHEET 2.9: THE NATURE AND IMPORTANCE OF TRANSPLANT SURGERY

Use pages 52–53 of the Student's Book to answer these questions:

1. What is transplant surgery?

2. What are the two types of transplant surgery?

3. What is ULTRA and why was it set up?

4. Why is transplant surgery important?

5. Would you be an organ donor? Give two reasons for your point of view.

6. Why may some people disagree with you?

WORKSHEET 2.10: DIFFERENT ATTITUDES TO TRANSPLANT SURGERY IN CHRISTIANITY

Use pages 54–55 of the Student's Book to answer these questions:

1. **Why do some Christians agree with transplant surgery as long as organs are not paid for?**

2. **Why do some Christians allow transplant only from living donors and only as long as the organ donors are not paid?**

3. **Why do some Christians not allow any form of transplant surgery?**

4. **Do you think the conjoined twins Jodie and Mary should have been separated? Give at least two reasons for your point of view.**

5. **Explain why some people may disagree with you.**

WORKSHEET 2.11: DIFFERENT ATTITUDES TO TRANSPLANT SURGERY IN ONE RELIGION OTHER THAN CHRISTIANITY

Use the Student's Book page 56 (Islam), page 57 (Judaism), page 58 (Hinduism) or page 59 (Sikhism) to answer these questions:

1. Explain why some Muslims/Jews/Hindus/Sikhs are against most forms of transplant surgery.

2. Explain why some Muslims/Jews/Hindus/Sikhs allow most forms of transplant surgery.

3. Do you think religious people should be allowed transplant surgery? Give at least three reasons.

4. Explain why some people may disagree with you.

APPENDIX 3

GENERIC LESSON PLAN AND WORKSHEETS FOR SECTION 3

Worksheets are provided for all the lessons in Section 3 (pages 66–88) along with a lesson plan (below) where most of the boxes have been left blank to enable you to adapt it for use with any of the worksheets.

LESSON PLAN

Lesson title
•

Lesson objectives	**Lesson outcomes**
•	•

Prior learning	**Resources**
•	• Student's Book pages xx–xx
	• Worksheet xx

5 mins	**Starter activity** Give out the worksheets and Student's Books, ensuring that everyone knows what they have to do.
25 mins	**Main activity** Ask students to complete Worksheet xx in pairs using the Student's Book pages xx–xx.
15 mins	**Plenary activity** Have a feedback session, going over the answers and ensuring that all students have amended their answers where necessary.

Extension Differentiation by outcome should be possible.	**Reinforcement** • Less able students should be paired with more able ones.

Homework •	**Assessment** •
	ICT •

WORKSHEET 3.1: THE UNITED NATIONS AND WORLD PEACE

Use pages 62–64 of the Student's Book to answer these questions:

1. What is the United Nations (UN)?

2. Why is the UN important for world peace?

3. Why did the UN become involved in Kosovo?

4. How has it dealt with the situation?

5. Do you think the UN is the best way to bring peace to the world? Give two reasons for your point of view.

6. Explain why some people may disagree with you.

WORKSHEET 3.2: HOW RELIGIOUS ORGANISATIONS TRY TO PROMOTE WORLD PEACE

Use page 65 of the Student's Book to answer these questions:

1. Name four religious organisations working for world peace.

2. What are the purposes of Pax Christi?

3. What are the main aims of the Muslim Peace Fellowship?

4. Explain how religious organisations work for world peace.

5. Do you think religious organisations are more likely to bring about world peace than the UN? Give at least three reasons.

6. Explain why some people may disagree with you.

WORKSHEET 3.3: WHY WARS OCCUR

Use pages 66–77 of the Student's Book to answer these questions:

1. How do current conflicts show religion as a cause of war?

2. How do current conflicts show nationalism and ethnicity as a cause of war?

3. How do current conflicts show economics as a cause of war?

4. How do current conflicts show ideology as a cause of war?

5. What did Goering claim was the major cause of war?

6. Do you think religion is the main cause of war? Give at least three reasons.

WORKSHEET 3.4: THE NATURE AND IMPORTANCE OF THE THEORY OF JUST WAR

Use page 68 of the Student's Book to answer these questions:

1. According to the just war theory, what would make a war a just war?

2. Where did the just war theory come from?

3. Do you think any modern war could be a just war? Give at least three reasons.

4. Explain why some people may disagree with you.

WORKSHEET 3.5: DIFFERENCES AMONG CHRISTIANS IN THEIR ATTITUDES TO WAR

Use pages 69–71 of the Student's Book to answer these questions:

1. What is Christian pacifism?

2. Why are some Christians pacifists?

3. Why do some Christians believe they can fight in just wars?

4. Do you think Christians can fight in modern wars? Give three reasons.

5. Explain why some people may disagree with you.

WORKSHEET 3.6A: THE ATTITUDES TO WAR OF ONE RELIGION OTHER THAN CHRISTIANITY

Use the Student's Book page 72 (Islam), page 73 (Judaism) or page 76 (Sikhism) to answer these questions:

1. What is the main attitude to war in Islam/Judaism/Sikhism?

2. What are the reasons for this attitude?

3. Why may some Muslims/Jews/Sikhs disagree with this attitude?

4. Do you think religious people should fight in wars? Give at least three reasons.

5. Explain why some people may disagree with you.

WORKSHEET 3.6B: HINDUISM AND ATTITUDES TO WAR

Use pages 74–75 of the Student's Book to answer these questions:

1. Why are some Hindus pacifists?

2. Why do some Hindus believe they can fight in just wars?

3. Do you think Hindus can fight in modern wars? Give three reasons.

4. Explain why some people may disagree with you.

WORKSHEET 3.7: CHRISTIAN ATTITUDES TO BULLYING

Use pages 77–78 of the Student's Book to answer these questions:

1. What is bullying?

2. What can the effects of bullying be?

3. Why are Christians against bullying? Give at least three reasons.

4. Explain why some Christian children may think their Christian parents are bullying them.

WORKSHEET 3.8: THE ATTITUDES TO BULLYING IN ONE RELIGION OTHER THAN CHRISTIANITY

Use the Student's Book page 79 (Islam), page 80 (Judaism), page 81 (Hinduism) or page 82 (Sikhism) to answer these questions:

1. Explain why Muslims/Jews/Hindus/Sikhs are against bullying. Give at least four reasons.

2. Why do you think Muslim/Jewish/Hindu/Sikh parents may be tempted to bully their children?

3. Do you think religious people should try to stop bullying when they see it happening? Give three reasons.

4. Why may some people disagree with you?

WORKSHEET 3.9: RELIGIOUS CONFLICTS WITHIN FAMILIES

Use pages 83–84 of the Student's Book to answer these questions:

1. How can children no longer wanting to take part in their parents' religion cause family conflicts?

2. How can children wanting to marry a partner from a different faith cause family conflicts?

3. How can children becoming more religious than their parents cause family conflicts?

4. How can disagreements over moral issues cause family conflicts?

5. Do you agree that religion causes more family conflicts than anything else? Give three reasons for your point of view.

6. Explain why some people may disagree with you.

WORKSHEET 3.10: CHRISTIAN TEACHINGS ON FORGIVENESS AND RECONCILIATION

Use page 85 of the Student's Book to answer these questions:

1. What does forgiveness mean?

2. What does reconciliation mean?

3. Why do Christians see forgiveness and reconciliation as the way to deal with conflicts between families and friends?

4. Do you agree that Christians should always forgive people? Give three reasons.

5. Explain why some people may disagree with you.

WORKSHEET 3.11: THE TEACHINGS ON FORGIVENESS AND RECONCILIATION OF ONE RELIGION OTHER THAN CHRISTIANITY

Use the Student's Book page 86 (Islam), page 87 (Judaism), page 88 (Hinduism) or page 89 (Sikhism) to answer these questions:

1. Write in your own words a quotation from a Muslim/Jewish/Hindu/Sikh holy book about forgiveness.

2. Why should Muslims/Jews/Hindus/Sikhs follow the teachings of their holy books?

3. Why do Muslims/Jews/Hindus/Sikhs see forgiveness and reconciliation as the way to deal with conflicts between families and friends?

4. Do you agree that Muslims/Jews/Hindus/Sikhs should always forgive people? Give three reasons.

5. Explain why some people may disagree with you.

APPENDIX 4

GENERIC LESSON PLAN AND WORKSHEETS FOR SECTION 4

Worksheets are provided for all the lessons in Section 4 (pages 89–119) along with a lesson plan (below) where most of the boxes have been left blank to enable you to adapt it for use with any of the worksheets.

LESSON PLAN

Lesson title
•

Lesson objectives	**Lesson outcomes**
•	•

Prior learning	**Resources**
•	• Student's Book pages xx–xx • Worksheet xx

5 mins	**Starter activity** Give out the worksheets and Student's Books, ensuring that everyone knows what they have to do.
25 mins	**Main activity** Ask students to complete Worksheet xx in pairs using the Student's Book pages xx–xx.
15 mins	**Plenary activity** Have a feedback session, going over the answers and ensuring that all students have amended their answers where necessary.

Extension Differentiation by outcome should be possible.	**Reinforcement** • Less able students should be paired with more able ones.
Homework •	**Assessment** •
	ICT •

WORKSHEET 4.1: THE NEED FOR LAW AND JUSTICE

Use pages 92–93 of the Student's Book to answer these questions:

1. What is law?

2. Give four reasons why we need laws.

3. What is a crime?

4. Which courts try crimes?

5. What is civil law?

6. Which courts try civil disputes?

7. Do you think there needs to be a connection between laws and justice? Give four reasons.

WORKSHEET 4.2: THEORIES OF PUNISHMENT

Use pages 94–95 of the Student's Book to answer these questions:

1. What is the retribution theory of punishment?

2. Why do some people think it is a good theory?

3. What is the deterrence theory of punishment?

4. Why do some people think it is a good theory?

5. What is the reform theory of punishment?

6. Why do some people think it is a good theory?

7. What is the protection theory of punishment?

8. Why do some people think it is a good theory?

WORKSHEET 4.3: WHY JUSTICE IS IMPORTANT FOR CHRISTIANS

Use pages 96–97 of the Student's Book to answer these questions:

1. Give five reasons why justice is important for Christians.

2. Why do you think there is a special chapel for justice and peace in Exeter Cathedral?

3. Why do you think Christians led the demonstrations for Fair Trade for LEDCs (poor countries)?

4. Do you think Christians should protect asylum seekers from being deported as Father Richard McKay did? Give two reasons for your point of view.

5. Explain why some people may disagree with you.

WORKSHEET 4.4: WHY JUSTICE IS IMPORTANT FOR THE FOLLOWERS OF ONE RELIGION OTHER THAN CHRISTIANITY

Use the Student's Book page 98 (Islam), page 99 (Judaism), page 100 (Hinduism) or page 101 (Sikhism) to answer these questions:

1. Give five reasons why justice is important for Muslims/Jews/Hindus/Sikhs.

2. Put one of the quotations on page 98/99/100/101 into your own words.

3. Put another of the quotations on page 98/99/100/101 into your own words.

4. Do you think justice is more important for religious people? Give two reasons for your point of view.

5. Explain why some people may disagree with you.

WORKSHEET 4.5: THE NATURE OF CAPITAL PUNISHMENT AND NON-RELIGIOUS ARGUMENTS ABOUT CAPITAL PUNISHMENT

Use the Student's Book pages 102–3 to answer these questions:

1. **What is capital punishment?**

2. **What crimes used to be punished by capital punishment?**

3. **What is the attitude of British law to capital punishment now?**

4. **Give four arguments in favour of capital punishment.**

5. **Give four arguments against capital punishment.**

6. **Do you think capital punishment would have been a better punishment for Harold Shipman than life imprisonment? Give two reasons for your point of view.**

WORKSHEET 4.6: DIFFERENT ATTITUDES TO CAPITAL PUNISHMENT AMONG CHRISTIANS

Use pages 104–5 of the Student's Book to answer these questions:

1. Give four reasons for Christians being against capital punishment.

2. Give four reasons for Christians allowing capital punishment.

3. Is the case of Timothy Evans an argument for or against capital punishment? Give your reasons.

4. Is the United Reformed Church in favour of capital punishment? Give your reasons.

WORKSHEET 4.7: DIFFERENT ATTITUDES TO CAPITAL PUNISHMENT IN ONE RELIGION OTHER THAN CHRISTIANITY

Use the Student's Book page 106 (Islam), page 107 (Judaism), page 108 (Hinduism) or page 109 (Sikhism) to answer these questions:

1. **Give three reasons for Muslims/Jews/Hindus/Sikhs being against capital punishment.**

2. **Give three reasons for Muslims/Jews/Hindus/Sikhs allowing capital punishment.**

3. **Do you think you can be really religious and be in favour of capital punishment? Give at least three reasons for your point of view.**

4. **Explain why some people may disagree with you.**

WORKSHEET 4.8: THE LAWS ON DRUGS AND ALCOHOL

Use pages 110–11 of the Student's Book to answer these questions:

1. Give four UK laws on tobacco.

2. Give four UK laws on alcohol.

3. Give four UK laws on drugs.

4. Do you think we need these laws? Give at least three reasons for your point of view.

WORKSHEET 4.9: SOCIAL AND HEALTH PROBLEMS CAUSED BY DRUGS AND ALCOHOL

Use the Student's Book pages 112–13 to answer these questions:

1. Give four health problems caused by tobacco.

2. What social problems are caused by tobacco?

3. Give four health problems caused by alcohol.

4. What social problems are caused by alcohol?

5. Give four health problems caused by drugs.

6. What social problems are caused by drugs?

WORKSHEET 4.10: DIFFERENT ATTITUDES TO DRUGS AND ALCOHOL IN CHRISTIANITY

Use pages 114–15 of the Student's Book to answer these questions:

1. Give three reasons to explain why all Christians are against illicit drug use.

2. Give three reasons to explain why many Christians believe moderation is the way Christians should use alcohol and/or tobacco.

3. Give three reasons to explain why some Christians believe Christians should never use alcohol and/or tobacco.

4. Use evidence from Topic 4.9, pages 112–13, to answer this question:

   The social and health problems of alcohol are so bad that it should be banned. Do you agree? Give three reasons.

5. Explain why some people may disagree with you.

WORKSHEET 4.11A: ATTITUDES TO DRUGS AND ALCOHOL IN ISLAM AND SIKHISM

Use the Student's Book page 116 (Islam) or page 119 (Sikhism) to answer these questions:

1. **Give five reasons why Muslims/Sikhs do not allow the use of drugs or alcohol.**

2. **Why do you think some Muslims/Sikhs use alcohol?**

3. **Why do you think some Muslims/Sikhs run shops selling alcohol?**

4. **Do you think the Muslim/Sikh attitude to drugs and alcohol is a good one? Give three reasons for your point of view.**

5. **Why may some people disagree with you?**

WORKSHEET 4.11B: ATTITUDES TO DRUGS AND ALCOHOL IN JUDAISM

Use the Student's Book page 117 to answer these questions:

1. Give three reasons to explain why all Jewish people are against illicit drug use.

2. What is the official Jewish attitude to tobacco?

3. What reasons are given in the margin for this attitude?

4. Give three reasons to explain why most Jewish people believe moderation is the way they should use alcohol.

5. Do you think the Jewish attitude to drugs and alcohol is a good one? Give three reasons for your point of view.

WORKSHEET 4.11C: ATTITUDES TO DRUGS AND ALCOHOL IN HINDUISM

Use the Student's Book page 118 to answer these questions:

1. Give four reasons why some Hindus do not allow the use of drugs, tobacco or alcohol.

2. Give three reasons why some Hindus allow the use of drugs, tobacco or alcohol in moderation.

3. If you were a Hindu, which attitude would you have? (You may wish to refer back to Topic 4.9.). Give at least three reasons.

4. Explain why some Hindus may disagree with you.

APPENDIX 5

EDEXCEL GENERIC MARK SCHEME

Question Number	Correct Answer	Partially Correct Answer	Reject	Mark
(a) AO1	Any alternative wording of the above points is acceptable. (2)	Any alternative wording of the above point is acceptable. (1)	Answers which define a different key word. (0)	2

Question Number	Indicative content	Mark
(b) AO2	**Award marks as follows:** For a personal response with: • one brief reason. **1 mark** For a personal response with: • two brief reasons • or one developed reason. **2 marks** For a personal response with: • two reasons with one developed. **3 marks** For a personal response with: • two developed reasons. **4 marks**	4

Question Number	Indicative content The quality of written communication will be assessed in this answer (strands i, ii and iii)	Mark
(c) AO1		8
Level	**Descriptor**	**Mark**
	No rewardable material.	0
Level 1	Little understanding of the issue is shown typically by: • giving a brief reason • not explaining but only describing the issue. The answer is likely to be in basic English. The skills needed to produce effective writing will not normally be present. The writing may have some coherence and will be generally comprehensible, but lack both clarity and organisation. High incidence of syntactical and/or spelling errors.	1–2
Level 2	Basic understanding of the issue is shown typically by: • giving two brief reasons • or a developed reason. The candidate is likely to express understanding with a limited command of English and little use of specialist vocabulary. The range of skills needed to produce effective writing is likely to be limited. There are likely to be passages which lack clarity and proper organisation. Frequent syntactical and/or spelling errors are likely to be present.	3–4

Level	Descriptor	Mark
Level 3	A more developed understanding of the issue is shown typically by: • using three brief reasons • or a fully developed reason • or two reasons with one developed. The candidate is likely to express understanding in a clear style of English and some use of specialist vocabulary. The candidate will demonstrate most of the skills needed to produce effective extended writing but there will be lapses in organisation. Some syntactical and/or spelling errors are likely to be present.	5–6
Level 4	A clear understanding of the issue is shown typically by: • using four brief reasons • or two developed reasons • or three reasons with one developed • or a comprehensive explanation using one reason only. The candidate is likely to express understanding in a clear and correct style of English with a correct use of specialist vocabulary where appropriate. The skills needed to produce convincing extended writing will be in place. Good organisation and clarity. Very few syntactical and/or spelling errors may be found. Excellent organisation and planning.	7–8

Question Number	Indicative content	Mark
(d) AO2	**Award marks as follows:** Candidates who do not refer to a religion in either (i) or (ii) cannot go beyond 3 marks for the whole of (d). (i) Own opinion **1 mark** for • a simple reason. **2 marks** for • a developed reason • or two simple reasons. **3 marks** for • three simple reasons • or two developed reasons • or a fully developed reason. (ii) Why some people may disagree with their opinion **1 mark** for • a simple reason. **2 marks** for • a developed reason • or two simple reasons. **3 marks** for • three simple reasons • or two developed reasons • or a fully developed reason.	6

APPENDIX 6 – MARK SCHEMES FOR END OF SECTION TESTS
MARK SCHEME FOR SECTION 1 TEST

Question Number	Correct Answer	Partially Correct Answer	Reject	Mark
1 (a) AO1	• the rights and freedoms to which everyone is entitled • the rights you have under the law **Any alternative wording of the above points is acceptable.** (2)	• everybody's rights **Any alternative wording of the above points is acceptable.** (1)	• answers which define a different key word. (0)	2

Question Number	Answer	Mark
1 (b) AO2	**Indicative content** Answers which think cloning is against God's will are likely to use such reasons as: • God has created the genetic make-up of each human being at the moment of conception and people have no right to interfere with God's will • genetic engineering is 'playing God', and that is a great sin • it is wrong to try to make the earth perfect, as only heaven is perfect Answers which think cloning is not against God's will are likely to use such reasons as: • Jesus was a healer who showed that Christians should do all they can to cure disease • discovering the genetic make-up of humans and using those discoveries to improve human life is part of what God wants humans to do as stewards of his creation • there is a difference between creating cells and creating people Other approaches are possible and must be marked according to the levels. **Award marks as follows:** For a personal response with: • one brief reason (e.g. it is playing God) **1 mark** For a personal response with: • two brief reasons • or one developed reason (e.g. it is playing God and playing God is a great sin) **2 marks** For a personal response with: • two reasons with one developed **3 marks** For a personal response with: • two developed reasons **4 marks**	4

Question Number	Indicative content The quality of written communication will be assessed in this answer (strands i, ii and iii)	Mark
1 (c) AO1	The main reasons are likely to be: • in the parable Jesus said that Christians should feed the hungry and clothe the naked, so Christians will want social change for the poor • in the parable Jesus said to invite in the stranger, so Christians will want social change for equal treatment of asylum seekers • in the parable Jesus said to visit the sick, so Christians will want social change for the sick and for their carers • in the parable Jesus said to visit those in prison, so Christians will want social change for prisoners Other approaches are possible and must be marked according to the levels. **Award marks as follows:**	8

Level	Descriptor	Mark
	No rewardable material.	0
Level 1	Little understanding of the issue is shown typically by: • giving a brief reason • not explaining but only describing the issue. The answer is likely to be in basic English. The skills needed to produce effective writing will not normally be present. The writing may have some coherence and will be generally comprehensible, but lack both clarity and organisation. High incidence of syntactical and/or spelling errors.	1–2
Level 2	Basic understanding of the issue is shown typically by: • giving two brief reasons • or a developed reason. The candidate is likely to express understanding with a limited command of English and little use of specialist vocabulary. The range of skills needed to produce effective writing is likely to be limited. There are likely to be passages which lack clarity and proper organisation. Frequent syntactical and/or spelling errors are likely to be present.	3–4
Level 3	A more developed understanding of the issue is shown typically by: • using three brief reasons • or a fully developed reason • or two reasons with one developed. The candidate is likely to express understanding in a clear style of English and some use of specialist vocabulary. The candidate will demonstrate most of the skills needed to produce effective extended writing but there will be lapses in organisation. Some syntactical and/or spelling errors are likely to be present.	5–6
Level 4	A clear understanding of the issue is shown typically by: • using four brief reasons • or two developed reasons • or three reasons with one developed • or a comprehensive explanation using one reason only. The candidate is likely to express understanding in a clear and correct style of English with a correct use of specialist vocabulary where appropriate. The skills needed to produce convincing extended writing will be in place. Good organisation and clarity. Very few syntactical and/or spelling errors may be found. Excellent organisation and planning.	7–8

Question Number	Answer	Mark
1 (d) AO2	**Indicative content** Reasons for supporting this statement could be: • Jesus over-ruled what the Old Testament said when he thought it was unloving: he said it was more important to do good than to obey the law not to work on the Sabbath • Jesus said that the only laws are to love God and love your neighbour • Christianity is a religion of love and forgiveness (as shown in the life and death of God's Son) and so Christians should make their moral decisions based on love not laws Reasons for not supporting this statement could be: • God would not have given laws in the Bible if they were not to be followed • some Christians believe they should follow what all other Christians agree is the right way to behave (e.g. the Ten Commandments and the Sermon on the Mount) rather than relying on their own ideas • some Christians think the Church knows better what Christians should do than the individual and so they follow the guidance of the Church Other approaches are possible and must be marked according to the levels. **Award marks as follows:** Candidates who do not refer to a religion in either (i) or (ii) cannot go beyond 3 marks for the whole of (d). (i) Own opinion **1 mark** for • a simple reason **2 marks** for • a developed reason • or two simple reasons **3 marks** for • three simple reasons • or two developed reasons • or a fully developed reason (ii) Why some people may disagree with their opinion **1 mark** for • a simple reason **2 marks** for • a developed reason • or two simple reasons **3 marks** for • three simple reasons • or two developed reasons • or a fully developed reason	6

Question Number	Correct Answer	Partially Correct Answer	Reject	Mark
2 (a) **AO1**	• a group formed to influence government policy on a particular issue • a group trying to change the law **Any alternative wording of the above points is acceptable.** (2)	• any example of a pressure group, e.g. the Green Party **Any alternative wording of the above point is acceptable.** (1)	• answers which define a different key word. (0)	2

Question Number	Answer	Mark
2 (b) **AO2**	**Indicative content** Answers which think conscience is the voice of God are likely to use such reasons as: • Christians believe that God speaks to Christians through their conscience, which is like a voice in people's heads telling them what they should or should not do • the Church says that conscience is the voice of God, and Christians are expected to follow the teachings of the Church • great Christian thinkers say that conscience is the voice of God Answers which think conscience is not the voice of God are likely to use such reasons as: • a voice in your head can be anything, there is no proof it is God • your conscience is just the moral values you have been brought up with • people have heard their conscience telling them to do evil things that God would never say Other approaches are possible and must be marked according to the levels. **Award marks as follows:** For a personal response with: • one brief reason (e.g. the Church says that it is)　　**1 mark** For a personal response with: • two brief reasons • or one developed reason (e.g. the Church says that it is, and Christians are expected to follow the teachings of the Church) 　　**2 marks** For a personal response with: • two reasons with one developed　　**3 marks** For a personal response with: • two developed reasons　　**4 marks**	4

Question Number	Indicative content The quality of written communication will be assessed in this answer (strands i, ii and iii)	Mark
2 (c) AO1	The main reasons are likely to be: • the right to life is important because we need to be protected from murder, from doctors being able to kill people for research, etc. • the right to liberty is important because people should not be slaves and people should not be arrested without good reason • the right to a fair trial is important because otherwise you could be imprisoned for something you did not do, as happens in countries without human rights laws • the right to participate in free elections is important because otherwise political leaders could manipulate elections to make themselves dictators Other approaches are possible and must be marked according to the levels. **Award marks as follows:**	8

Level	Descriptor	Mark
	No rewardable material.	0
Level 1	Little understanding of the issue is shown typically by: • giving a brief reason • not explaining but only describing the issue. The answer is likely to be in basic English. The skills needed to produce effective writing will not normally be present. The writing may have some coherence and will be generally comprehensible, but lack both clarity and organisation. High incidence of syntactical and/or spelling errors.	1–2
Level 2	Basic understanding of the issue is shown typically by: • giving two brief reasons • or a developed reason. The candidate is likely to express understanding with a limited command of English and little use of specialist vocabulary. The range of skills needed to produce effective writing is likely to be limited. There are likely to be passages which lack clarity and proper organisation. Frequent syntactical and/or spelling errors are likely to be present.	3–4
Level 3	A more developed understanding of the issue is shown typically by: • using three brief reasons • or a fully developed reason • or two reasons with one developed. The candidate is likely to express understanding in a clear style of English and some use of specialist vocabulary. The candidate will demonstrate most of the skills needed to produce effective extended writing but there will be lapses in organisation. Some syntactical and/or spelling errors are likely to be present.	5–6
Level 4	A clear understanding of the issue is shown typically by: • using four brief reasons • or two developed reasons • or three reasons with one developed • or a comprehensive explanation using one reason only. The candidate is likely to express understanding in a clear and correct style of English with a correct use of specialist vocabulary where appropriate. The skills needed to produce convincing extended writing will be in place. Good organisation and clarity. Very few syntactical and/or spelling errors may be found. Excellent organisation and planning.	7–8

Question Number	Answer	Mark
2 (d) **AO2**	**Indicative content** Reasons for supporting this statement could be: • you are only one person out of 60 million so your vote makes no difference • all politicians are the same so it doesn't matter which you vote for • political parties do not do what they say in elections so it's a waste of time voting Reasons for not supporting this statement could be: • the national Government sets the rates of tax and collects the taxes so voting gives you some control over this • the Government can pass new laws that will affect your life and voting gives you a chance to affect these laws • voting gives you a say in how things like the NHS, the Police, etc. are run Other approaches are possible and must be marked according to the levels. **Award marks as follows:** (i) Own opinion **1 mark** for • a simple reason **2 marks** for • a developed reason • or two simple reasons **3 marks** for • three simple reasons • or two developed reasons • or a fully developed reason (ii) Why some people may disagree with their opinion **1 mark** for • a simple reason **2 marks** for • a developed reason • or two simple reasons **3 marks** for • three simple reasons • or two developed reasons • or a fully developed reason	6

MARK SCHEME FOR SECTION 2 TEST

Question Number	Correct Answer	Partially Correct Answer	Reject	Mark
1 (a) AO1	• giving organs to be used in transplant surgery **Any alternative wording of the above point is acceptable.** (2)	• giving organs **Any alternative wording of the above point is acceptable.** (1)	• answers which define a different key word (0)	2

Question Number	Answer	Mark
1 (b) AO2	**Indicative content** Answers which think children have a right to know their donors are likely to use such reasons as: • it is a basic human right to know your genetic ancestry • UK law says that children have the right to know their donors when they are 18 • if you don't know your donor, then you could end up marrying a half-brother or half-sister Answers which think children do not have a right to know their donors are likely to use such reasons as: • people will not donate sperm and eggs if they think children might knock on their door in 18 years' time • it could cause family problems if donors intervened in family life • it is bringing up children that makes a parent, not giving sperm or eggs Other approaches are possible and must be marked according to the levels. **Award marks as follows:** For a personal response with: • one brief reason (e.g. it is the law) **1 mark** For a personal response with: • two brief reasons • or one developed reason (e.g. it is the law, and children have a right to know their donors) **2 marks** For a personal response with: • two reasons with one developed **3 marks** For a personal response with: • two developed reasons **4 marks**	4

Question Number	Indicative content The quality of written communication will be assessed in this answer (strands i, ii and iii)	Mark
1 (c) AO1	**Hinduism, for example:** Many Hindus accept all forms of infertility treatment because: • these are simply using medicine to bring about the family life which all Hindus are expected to have to fulfil the householder stage of life	8

Question Number	Indicative content The quality of written communication will be assessed in this answer (strands i, ii and iii)	Mark
1 (c) AO1	• the egg and sperm are from the husband and wife and so the baby will be the biological offspring of its mother and father • the Laws of Manu encourage infertile couples to adopt from a relative, which is no different from infertility treatments Some Hindus do not allow AID, egg donation or surrogacy because: • they believe caste is passed down through the parents and so the child could be a different caste from the parents • IVF involves fertilising several eggs, some of which are thrown away or used for experimentation. Such Hindus believe that once an embryo has been created, it is alive and so cannot then be deliberately killed • they see AID and egg donation as a form of adultery, which is banned by Hinduism Other approaches are possible and must be marked according to the levels. **Award marks as follows:**	8

Level	Descriptor	Mark
	No rewardable material.	0
Level 1	Little understanding of the issue is shown typically by: • giving a brief reason • not explaining but only describing the issue. The answer is likely to be in basic English. The skills needed to produce effective writing will not normally be present. The writing may have some coherence and will be generally comprehensible, but lack both clarity and organisation. High incidence of syntactical and/or spelling errors.	1–2
Level 2	Basic understanding of the issue is shown typically by: • giving two brief reasons • or a developed reason. The candidate is likely to express understanding with a limited command of English and little use of specialist vocabulary. The range of skills needed to produce effective writing is likely to be limited. There are likely to be passages which lack clarity and proper organisation. Frequent syntactical and/or spelling errors are likely to be present.	3–4
Level 3	A more developed understanding of the issue is shown typically by: • using three brief reasons • or a fully developed reason • or two reasons with one developed. The candidate is likely to express understanding in a clear style of English and some use of specialist vocabulary. The candidate will demonstrate most of the skills needed to produce effective extended writing but there will be lapses in organisation. Some syntactical and/or spelling errors are likely to be present.	5–6

Level	Descriptor	Mark
Level 4	A clear understanding of the issue is shown typically by: • using four brief reasons • or two developed reasons • or three reasons with one developed • or a comprehensive explanation using one reason only. The candidate is likely to express understanding in a clear and correct style of English with a correct use of specialist vocabulary where appropriate. The skills needed to produce convincing extended writing will be in place. Good organisation and clarity. Very few syntactical and/or spelling errors may be found. Excellent organisation and planning.	7–8

Question Number	Answer	Mark
1 (d) **AO2**	**Indicative content** Reasons for supporting this statement could be: • the responsibility to be God's stewards and to leave the Earth a better place than they found it means that Christians should try to reduce pollution and preserve resources for future generations • the belief that stewardship means a fair sharing of the Earth's resources means that Christians should try to improve the quality of life of the less fortunate by sharing the Earth's resources more fairly without causing more pollution • the belief that, after death, they will be judged by God on their behaviour as stewards means that many Christians feel they have a duty to share in and support the work of groups which try to reduce pollution and conserve resources Reasons for not supporting this statement could be: • at least half of the world's population is not Christian and so they would not be following the teachings • problems like scarce resources can only be solved by science and governments finding new ways of providing energy, producing similar products to steel, etc. • problems like nuclear waste cannot be solved by stewardship Other approaches are possible and must be marked according to the levels. **Award marks as follows:** Candidates who do not refer to a religion in either (i) or (ii) cannot go beyond 3 marks for the whole of (d). (i) Own opinion **1 mark** for • a simple reason **2 marks** for • a developed reason • or two simple reasons **3 marks** for • three simple reasons • or two developed reasons • or a fully developed reason	6

Question Number	Answer	Mark
1 (d) AO2	(ii) Why some people may disagree with their opinion **1 mark** for • a simple reason **2 marks** for • a developed reason • or two simple reasons **3 marks** for • three simple reasons • or two developed reasons • or a fully developed reason	6

Question Number	Correct Answer	Partially Correct Answer	Reject	Mark
2 (a) AO1	• an arrangement whereby a woman bears a child on behalf of another woman • where an egg is donated and fertilised by the husband through IVF and then implanted into the wife's uterus **Any alternative wording of the above points is acceptable.** (2)	• egg donation **Any alternative wording of the above point is acceptable.** (1)	• answers which define a different key word (0)	2

Question Number	Answer	Mark
2 (b) AO2	**Indicative content** Answers which think global warming is a problem are likely to use such reasons as: • it will lead to the ice caps melting, which would flood coastal areas • it could lead to countries like Spain becoming deserts • it could lead to less land being available for farming and so lead to famines Answers which think global warming is not a problem are likely to use such reasons as: • it will increase temperatures and make places like Greenland more attractive to live in • it will make it easier to grow crops in some countries, e.g. grapes in the UK • we have the technology to deal with any problems caused by global warming Other approaches are possible and must be marked according to the levels.	4

Question Number	Answer	Mark
2 (b) AO2	**Award marks as follows:** For a personal response with: • one brief reason (e.g. it will lead to the ice caps melting) **1 mark** For a personal response with: • two brief reasons • or one developed reason (e.g. it will lead to the ice caps melting, which would flood coastal areas) **2 marks** For a personal response with: • two reasons with one developed **3 marks** For a personal response with: • two developed reasons **4 marks**	4

Question Number	Indicative content The quality of written communication will be assessed in this answer (strands i, ii and iii)	Mark
2(c) AO1	**Islam, for example:** The main reasons are likely to be: • the responsibility to be God's khalifah means that Muslims should try to reduce pollution and preserve resources by following the Shari'ah • the Shari'ah and the ummah make many Muslims believe that stewardship means a fair sharing of the Earth's resources without causing more pollution • the belief in life as a test, with judgement on their behaviour as khalifahs, means that many Muslims feel they have a duty to share in and support the work of groups that try to reduce pollution and conserve resources • the belief in final judgement means that every Muslim should be judging what they are doing in their life as an individual by the standards of Islamic stewardship • there is a unity and balance in creation, therefore Muslims have a duty to preserve the environment and to make sure that it continues to be what God intended it to be Other approaches are possible and must be marked according to the levels. **Award marks as follows:**	8

Level	Descriptor	Mark
	No rewardable material.	0
Level 1	Little understanding of the issue is shown typically by: • giving a brief reason • not explaining but only describing the issue. The answer is likely to be in basic English. The skills needed to produce effective writing will not normally be present. The writing may have some coherence and will be generally comprehensible, but lack both clarity and organisation. High incidence of syntactical and/or spelling errors.	1–2
Level 2	Basic understanding of the issue is shown typically by: • giving two brief reasons • or a developed reason. The candidate is likely to express understanding with a limited command of English and little use of specialist vocabulary. The range of skills needed to produce effective writing is likely to be limited. There are likely to be passages which lack clarity and proper organisation. Frequent syntactical and/or spelling errors are likely to be present.	3–4

Level	Descriptor	Mark
Level 3	A more developed understanding of the issue is shown typically by: • using three brief reasons • or a fully developed reason • or two reasons with one developed. The candidate is likely to express understanding in a clear style of English and some use of specialist vocabulary. The candidate will demonstrate most of the skills needed to produce effective extended writing but there will be lapses in organisation. Some syntactical and/or spelling errors are likely to be present.	5–6
Level 4	A clear understanding of the issue is shown typically by: • using four brief reasons • or two developed reasons • or three reasons with one developed • or a comprehensive explanation using one reason only. The candidate is likely to express understanding in a clear and correct style of English with a correct use of specialist vocabulary where appropriate. The skills needed to produce convincing extended writing will be in place. Good organisation and clarity. Very few syntactical and/or spelling errors may be found. Excellent organisation and planning.	7–8

Question Number	Answer	Mark
2 (d) AO2	**Indicative content** Reasons for supporting this statement could be: • having children and raising a Christian family is one of the purposes of Christian marriage • the Bible says that people were created to marry and have children • in a religion like Hinduism, you cannot achieve moksha if you do not marry and have children Reasons for not supporting this statement could be: • the Catholic view is that life is given by God and that no one has a right to have children • although the Catholic Church feels great sympathy for the childless who want children, it only allows methods which do not threaten the sacredness of life and in which sex acts are natural • many Christians believe they are called to serve God in other ways than having children Other approaches are possible and must be marked according to the levels. **Award marks as follows:** Candidates who do not refer to a religion in either (i) or (ii) cannot go beyond 3 marks for the whole of (d). (i) Own opinion **1 mark** for • a simple reason **2 marks** for • a developed reason • or two simple reasons **3 marks** for • three simple reasons • or two developed reasons • or a fully developed reason (ii) Why some people may disagree with their opinion **1 mark** for • a simple reason **2 marks** for • a developed reason • or two simple reasons **3 marks** for • three simple reasons • or two developed reasons • or a fully developed reason	6

MARK SCHEME FOR SECTION 3 TEST

Question Number	Correct Answer	Partially Correct Answer	Reject	Mark
1 (a) AO1	• bringing a fight or struggle to a peaceful conclusion • bringing two sides in a fight together **Any alternative wording of the above points is acceptable.** (2)	• ending wars **Any alternative wording of the above point is acceptable.** (1)	• answers which define a different key word (0)	2

Question Number	Answer	Mark
1 (b) AO2	**Indicative content** Answers which think you should always forgive others are likely to use such reasons as: • when Peter asked if he should forgive his brother up to seven times, Jesus told him that he should forgive up to seventy-seven times • Jesus said that if people do not forgive those who have sinned against them, God will not forgive their sins • St Paul said that Christians should try to live in peace with everyone. The only way to live in peace with everyone is to try to bring about reconciliation through forgiving those who wrong you Answers which think you should not always forgive others are likely to use such reasons as: • some crimes are too bad to be forgiven, for example, abusing children • if you forgive criminals they will just keep doing the same evil things • some people cannot even forgive themselves if they cause harm, such as if your child is killed because you crashed the car Other approaches are possible and must be marked according to the levels. **Award marks as follows:** For a personal response with: • one brief reason (e.g. some crimes are too bad to be forgiven) **1 mark** For a personal response with: • two brief reasons • or one developed reason (e.g. some crimes are too bad to be forgiven, such as abusing children) **2 marks** For a personal response with: • two reasons with one developed **3 marks** For a personal response with: • two developed reasons **4 marks**	4

Question Number	Indicative content The quality of written communication will be assessed in this answer (strands i, ii and iii)	Mark
1 (c) AO1	The main ways are likely to be: • placing violence-reduction teams of pacifist believers into crisis situations and militarised areas around the world at the invitation of local peace and human rights workers • sending trained, skilled, international teams of believers to support local efforts toward non-violent peacemaking • trying to stop the injustice which causes conflict through direct non-violent intervention, public witness and reporting to the larger world community • organising public debates on wars and conflicts and engaging congregations, meetings and support groups to play a key advocacy role with policy makers • making public statements about war, such as condemning the Iraq War and American intervention in Afghanistan • organising and attending inter-faith conferences to help all religions work together to promote world peace Other approaches are possible and must be marked according to the levels. **Award marks as follows:**	8

Level	Descriptor	Mark
	No rewardable material.	0
Level 1	Little understanding of the issue is shown typically by: • giving a brief reason • not explaining but only describing the issue. The answer is likely to be in basic English. The skills needed to produce effective writing will not normally be present. The writing may have some coherence and will be generally comprehensible, but lack both clarity and organisation. High incidence of syntactical and/or spelling errors.	1–2
Level 2	Basic understanding of the issue is shown typically by: • giving two brief reasons • or a developed reason. The candidate is likely to express understanding with a limited command of English and little use of specialist vocabulary. The range of skills needed to produce effective writing is likely to be limited. There are likely to be passages which lack clarity and proper organisation. Frequent syntactical and/or spelling errors are likely to be present.	3–4
Level 3	A more developed understanding of the issue is shown typically by: • using three brief reasons • or a fully developed reason • or two reasons with one developed. The candidate is likely to express understanding in a clear style of English and some use of specialist vocabulary. The candidate will demonstrate most of the skills needed to produce effective extended writing but there will be lapses in organisation. Some syntactical and/or spelling errors are likely to be present.	5–6
Level 4	A clear understanding of the issue is shown typically by: • using four brief reasons • or two developed reasons • or three reasons with one developed • or a comprehensive explanation using one reason only. The candidate is likely to express understanding in a clear and correct style of English with a correct use of specialist vocabulary where appropriate. The skills needed to produce convincing extended writing will be in place. Good organisation and clarity. Very few syntactical and/or spelling errors may be found. Excellent organisation and planning.	7–8

Question Number	Answer	Mark
1 (d) AO2	**Indicative content** Reasons for supporting this statement could be: • if parents are religious and go regularly to church/mosque/mandir/synagogue/gurdwara, they will expect their children to go with them. If their children refuse when they reach their teens, this can cause major conflict • children wanting to marry someone from a different religion can cause major conflict because they have betrayed their roots and family by falling in love with someone from a different religion • religion can cause children to criticise the lifestyle of the parents: for example, Catholic parents who use contraception; Muslim parents who run off-licences and sell national lottery tickets; Hindu parents who eat beef Reasons for not supporting this statement could be: • religion is often what keeps a family together as they join together for worship and festivals • there are many non-religious families where religion is never a cause of conflict • things like money and politics cause more conflicts in families than religion does Other approaches are possible and must be marked according to the levels. **Award marks as follows:** Candidates who do not refer to a religion in either (i) or (ii) cannot go beyond 3 marks for the whole of (d). (i) Own opinion **1 mark** for • a simple reason **2 marks** for • a developed reason • or two simple reasons **3 marks** for • three simple reasons • or two developed reasons • or a fully developed reason (ii) Why some people may disagree with their opinion **1 mark** for • a simple reason **2 marks** for • a developed reason • or two simple reasons **3 marks** for • three simple reasons • or two developed reasons • or a fully developed reason	6

Question Number	Correct Answer	Partially Correct Answer	Reject	Mark
2 (a) AO1	• taking advantage of a weaker group • using a stronger position to cheat the weak **Any alternative wording of the above points is acceptable.** (2)	• cheating the poor **Any alternative wording of the above point is acceptable.** (1)	• answers which define a different key word (0)	2

Question Number	Answer	Mark
2 (b) AO2	**Indicative content** Answers which think Christians can be bullies are likely to use such reasons as: • parents forcing their children to go to worship with them • religious leaders bullying their congregations by threatening them with punishment after death • parents banning their children from doing things they want to do because they are unChristian Answers which think Christians are never bullies are likely to use such reasons as: • Christianity regards using violence without a just cause as sinful, and bullying always involves using violence, which is unjustified and so is sinful • Christianity teaches that human beings are a creation of God made in God's image. Bullying is mistreating God's creation and so is wrong • the Church teaches that bullying is wrong as it is the duty of Christians to protect the weak and innocent Other approaches are possible and must be marked according to the levels. **Award marks as follows:** For a personal response with: • one brief reason (e.g. the Church teaches that bullying is wrong) **1 mark** For a personal response with: • two brief reasons • or one developed reason (e.g. the Church teaches that bullying is wrong as it is the duty of Christians to protect the weak and innocent) **2 marks** For a personal response with: • two reasons with one developed **3 marks** For a personal response with: • two developed reasons **4 marks**	4

Question Number	Indicative content The quality of written communication will be assessed in this answer (strands i, ii and iii)	Mark
2 (c) **AO1**	The main reasons are likely to be: • If parents are religious and go regularly to church or mosque or mandir or synagogue or gurdwara, they will expect their children to go with them. If their children refuse when they reach their teens, this can cause major conflict because: religions usually tell parents that it is their duty to bring their children up in the faith and ensure they become full members of it as adults; therefore if the children no longer take part in the religion, their parents will be regarded as failures by other believers and will worry that their children will not be with them in the after-life because they have left the faith. Children will feel that their human right to freedom of religion (which includes the freedom not to believe) is being taken away by their parents. • Children wanting to marry someone from a different religion can raise many problems for religious parents and religious leaders because: there can be no religious wedding ceremony; which religion the children of the marriage will be brought up in; for the parents and relatives of the couple there is often the feeling that they have betrayed their roots and family by falling in love with someone from a different religion. • Often parents are members of a religion, but not very strictly. If their children then become strict followers of the religion it can cause major conflict as parents get angry if their children criticise them, especially when the children have religion on their side. If the child wants to have a low paid job as a priest (minister), imam, charity worker, or join a religious community after their parents have spent a lot of money on their university education, the parents will often be angry. There can be conflict if the child criticises the lifestyle of the parents, for example, Catholic parents who use contraception, Muslim parents who run off-licences and sell lottery tickets, or Hindu parents who eat beef. Other approaches are possible and must be marked according to the levels. **Award marks as follows:**	8

Level	Descriptor	Mark
	No rewardable material.	0
Level 1	Little understanding of the issue is shown typically by: • giving a brief reason • not explaining but only describing the issue. The answer is likely to be in basic English. The skills needed to produce effective writing will not normally be present. The writing may have some coherence and will be generally comprehensible, but lack both clarity and organisation. High incidence of syntactical and/or spelling errors.	1–2
Level 2	Basic understanding of the issue is shown typically by: • giving two brief reasons • or a developed reason. The candidate is likely to express understanding with a limited command of English and little use of specialist vocabulary. The range of skills needed to produce effective writing is likely to be limited. There are likely to be passages which lack clarity and proper organisation. Frequent syntactical and/or spelling errors are likely to be present.	3–4
Level 3	A more developed understanding of the issue is shown typically by: • using three brief reasons • or a fully developed reason • or two reasons with one developed. The candidate is likely to express understanding in a clear style of English and some use of specialist vocabulary. The candidate will demonstrate most of the skills needed to produce effective extended writing but there will be lapses in organisation. Some syntactical and/or spelling errors are likely to be present.	5–6
Level 4	A clear understanding of the issue is shown typically by: • using four brief reasons • or two developed reasons • or three reasons with one developed • or a comprehensive explanation using one reason only. The candidate is likely to express understanding in a clear and correct style of English with a correct use of specialist vocabulary where appropriate. The skills needed to produce convincing extended writing will be in place. Good organisation and clarity. Very few syntactical and/or spelling errors may be found. Excellent organisation and planning.	7–8

Question Number	Answer	Mark
2 (d) AO2	**Indicative content** Reasons for supporting this statement could include the following examples of wars caused by religion: • the war in Bosnia and Kosovo, where the Serbian army ostensibly invaded because their fellow Orthodox Christians were being badly treated by the Muslim majority • the war in Kashmir, where the Muslims of Kashmir are fighting to leave Hindu India and become part of the Muslim state of Pakistan • the wars where there are differences within a religion and one religious group attacks the other for having different beliefs, for example, Iraq, Afghanistan, Northern Ireland Reasons for not supporting this statement could be: • many wars are caused by nationalism, for example, the First World War, the Tamil Tigers in Sri Lanka • many wars are caused by ideological differences, for example, the Second World War, the Congo • many wars are caused by economic problems Other approaches are possible and must be marked according to the levels. **Award marks as follows:** Candidates who do not refer to a religion in either (i) or (ii) cannot go beyond 3 marks for the whole of (d). (i) Own opinion **1 mark** for • a simple reason **2 marks** for • a developed reason • or two simple reasons **3 marks** for • three simple reasons • or two developed reasons • or a fully developed reason (ii) Why some people may disagree with their opinion **1 mark** for • a simple reason **2 marks** for • a developed reason • or two simple reasons **3 marks** for • three simple reasons • or two developed reasons • or a fully developed reason	6

Religion and Society Teacher's Resource Pack Third Edition © Hodder Education, 2009

MARK SCHEME FOR SECTION 4 TEST

Question Number	Correct Answer	Partially Correct Answer	Reject	Mark
1 (a) AO1	• a recurring compulsion to engage in an activity regardless of its bad effects • when you can't do without a drug, for example, alcoholics or heroin addicts **Any alternative wording of the above points is acceptable.** (2)	• an example of addiction, such as alcoholism **Any alternative wording of the above point is acceptable.** (1)	• answers which define a different key word (0)	2

Question Number	Answer	Mark
1 (b) AO2	**Indicative content** Answers which think religious people should support capital punishment are likely to use such reasons as: • the Bible sets down the death penalty as the punishment for a number of crimes, so it is allowed by God • for Muslims it is a punishment set down by God in the Qur'an and Muslims believe the Qur'an is the word of God • the Roman Catholic Church and the Church of England have not retracted their statements that permit the state to use capital punishment Answers which think religious people should not support capital punishment are likely to use such reasons as: • Christianity is based on the belief that Jesus came to save (reform) sinners. It is impossible to reform a criminal who has been executed • Jesus banned retribution when he said that an eye for an eye and a tooth for a tooth is wrong • Christianity teaches that human life is sacred and that only God has the right to take life Other approaches are possible and must be marked according to the levels. **Award marks as follows:** For a personal response with: • one brief reason (e.g. Christianity teaches that human life is sacred) **1 mark** For a personal response with: • two brief reasons • or one developed reason (e.g. Christianity teaches that human life is sacred and that only God has the right to take life) **2 marks** For a personal response with: • two reasons with one developed **3 marks** For a personal response with: • two developed reasons **4 marks**	4

Question Number	Indicative content The quality of written communication will be assessed in this answer (strands i, ii and iii)	Mark
1 (c) AO1	**Islam, for example:** Islam teaches that alcohol and drugs are prohibited for Muslims (haram) because: • the Qur'an says that intoxicants are a means by which Satan tries to keep people from God and from saying their prayers, and so Muslims should abstain from them • the Prophet Muhammad said that every intoxicant (anything which clouds the mind or changes perception and reasoning) is khamr and every khamr is forbidden to Muslims • Islam forbids its followers from committing suicide, and Muslim lawyers equate taking drugs or alcohol as a form of suicide because you are harming your body • Muslim lawyers take Muhammad's statement 'Do not harm yourselves or others' to mean that alcohol and all illegal drugs are forbidden because they all harm the body • Muhammad said on several occasions that not only must Muslims not drink alcohol, they must have nothing to do with the production or sale of alcohol • it is reported that when a Muslim came to Muhammad and said he had been given a cask of wine and asked if he could sell it, the Prophet opened the cask and let all the wine soak into the ground, saying that Muslims should have nothing to do with alcohol at all Other approaches are possible and must be marked according to the levels. **Award marks as follows:**	8

Level	Descriptor	Mark
	No rewardable material.	0
Level 1	Little understanding of the issue is shown typically by: • giving a brief reason • not explaining but only describing the issue. The answer is likely to be in basic English. The skills needed to produce effective writing will not normally be present. The writing may have some coherence and will be generally comprehensible, but lack both clarity and organisation. High incidence of syntactical and/or spelling errors.	1–2
Level 2	Basic understanding of the issue is shown typically by: • giving two brief reasons • or a developed reason. The candidate is likely to express understanding with a limited command of English and little use of specialist vocabulary. The range of skills needed to produce effective writing is likely to be limited. There are likely to be passages which lack clarity and proper organisation. Frequent syntactical and/or spelling errors are likely to be present.	3–4
Level 3	A more developed understanding of the issue is shown typically by: • using three brief reasons • or a fully developed reason • or two reasons with one developed. The candidate is likely to express understanding in a clear style of English and some use of specialist vocabulary. The candidate will demonstrate most of the skills needed to produce effective extended writing but there will be lapses in organisation. Some syntactical and/or spelling errors are likely to be present.	5–6
Level 4	A clear understanding of the issue is shown typically by: • using four brief reasons • or two developed reasons • or three reasons with one developed • or a comprehensive explanation using one reason only. The candidate is likely to express understanding in a clear and correct style of English with a correct use of specialist vocabulary where appropriate. The skills needed to produce convincing extended writing will be in place. Good organisation and clarity. Very few syntactical and/or spelling errors may be found. Excellent organisation and planning.	7–8

Question Number	Answer	Mark
1 (d) AO2	**Indicative content** Reasons for supporting this statement could be: • Christians have to be interested in justice because the Bible says that God is just and will reward the good and punish the evil, if not in this life, then in the world to come • the Bible says that people should be treated fairly and not cheated, and that God wants the world to be ruled justly and so they believe that Christians should be concerned about justice • the Christian Churches have made many statements about the need for Christians to work for justice and fairness in the world Reasons for not supporting this statement could be: • everyone is concerned about justice because if there is no justice, people will feel that it is right to break the law, and if people feel it is right to break laws then the whole basis of society may disintegrate • all people need justice to make sure that people are rewarded for their work, the weak are protected, etc. • if there is no justice in a society, people will think the society is not working and may start a civil war (e.g. Bosnia, Kosovo) Other approaches are possible and must be marked according to the levels. **Award marks as follows:** Candidates who do not refer to a religion in either (i) or (ii) cannot go beyond 3 marks for the whole of (d). (i) Own opinion **1 mark** for • a simple reason **2 marks** for • a developed reason • or two simple reasons **3 marks** for • three simple reasons • or two developed reasons • or a fully developed reason (ii) Why some people may disagree with their opinion **1 mark** for • a simple reason **2 marks** for • a developed reason • or two simple reasons **3 marks** for • three simple reasons • or two developed reasons • or a fully developed reason	6

Question Number	Correct Answer	Partially Correct Answer	Reject	Mark
2 (a) AO1	• restoring to normal life • getting someone back from addiction to a normal life **Any alternative wording of the above points is acceptable.** (2)	• ending addiction **Any alternative wording of the above point is acceptable.** (1)	• answers which define a different key word (0)	2

Question Number	Answer	Mark

2 (b) AO2	**Indicative content**
	Answers which think we need laws are likely to use such reasons as:
	• human beings live in groups, and any group needs rules to organise the behaviour of individuals
	• imagine what the roads would be like if there were no laws: people would be able to drive on whichever side of the road they liked; people would be able to drive at any speed they liked; there could be no traffic lights because drivers would not need to obey them; therefore we need laws so that people know what sort of behaviour to expect from each other
	• we need laws to protect the weak from the strong: imagine what life would be like if there were no laws on stealing, murder and rape
	
	Answers which think we do not need laws are likely to use such reasons as:
	• people are basically good and we would all treat each other in a way which would make life work
	• laws are made by the rich to keep the poor poor
	• laws do not stop people from murdering, etc.
	
	Other approaches are possible and must be marked according to the levels.
	
	Award marks as follows:
	For a personal response with:
	• one brief reason (e.g. because human beings live in groups)
	    1 mark
	
	For a personal response with:
	• two brief reasons
	• or one developed reason (e.g. because human beings live in groups, and any group needs rules to organise the behaviour of individuals)
	    2 marks
	
	For a personal response with:
	• two reasons with one developed **3 marks**
	For a personal response with:
	• two developed reasons **4 marks**
		4

Question Number	Indicative content The quality of written communication will be assessed in this answer (strands i, ii and iii)	Mark
2 (c) AO1	**Islam, for example:** The main reasons are likely to be: • Muhammad made several statements agreeing with capital punishment for murder, adultery and apostasy, and Muslims believe that Muhammad is the seal of the prophets whose words should be obeyed • Muhammad sentenced people to death for murder when he was ruler of Madinah, and Muslims believe Muhammad is the final exemplar whose example should be followed • the Sharia'h says that capital punishment is the punishment for murder, adultery and apostasy, and Muslims are expected to follow the holy law of Islam • the Qur'an supports capital punishment for certain crimes, and the Qur'an is the word of God for Muslims Other approaches are possible and must be marked according to the levels. **Award marks as follows:**	8

Level	Descriptor	Mark
	No rewardable material.	0
Level 1	Little understanding of the issue is shown typically by: • giving a brief reason • not explaining but only describing the issue. The answer is likely to be in basic English. The skills needed to produce effective writing will not normally be present. The writing may have some coherence and will be generally comprehensible, but lack both clarity and organisation. High incidence of syntactical and/or spelling errors.	1–2
Level 2	Basic understanding of the issue is shown typically by: • giving two brief reasons • or a developed reason. The candidate is likely to express understanding with a limited command of English and little use of specialist vocabulary. The range of skills needed to produce effective writing is likely to be limited. There are likely to be passages which lack clarity and proper organisation. Frequent syntactical and/or spelling errors are likely to be present.	3–4
Level 3	A more developed understanding of the issue is shown typically by: • using three brief reasons • or a fully developed reason • or two reasons with one developed. The candidate is likely to express understanding in a clear style of English and some use of specialist vocabulary. The candidate will demonstrate most of the skills needed to produce effective extended writing but there will be lapses in organisation. Some syntactical and/or spelling errors are likely to be present.	5–6
Level 4	A clear understanding of the issue is shown typically by: • using four brief reasons • or two developed reasons • or three reasons with one developed • or a comprehensive explanation using one reason only. The candidate is likely to express understanding in a clear and correct style of English with a correct use of specialist vocabulary where appropriate. The skills needed to produce convincing extended writing will be in place. Good organisation and clarity. Very few syntactical and/or spelling errors may be found. Excellent organisation and planning.	7–8

Question Number	Answer	Mark
2 (d) **AO2**	**Indicative content** Reasons for supporting this statement could be: • there is no proof that a drug like cannabis harms the user • people who take drugs like cannabis become peaceful and happy and so cause no harm • lots of people in British society take drugs and cause no harm Reasons for not supporting this statement could be: • the physical health of drug users can be damaged by toxic effects of a drug, dependence, or the way it is used (such as infection with a dirty needle) • the heavy cost of maintaining a heroin or cocaine habit forces users into a life of crime, where they harm other people by stealing from them • some users become violent under a drug's influence and harm those around them Other approaches are possible and must be marked according to the levels. **Award marks as follows:** Candidates who do not refer to a religion in either (i) or (ii) cannot go beyond 3 marks for the whole of (d). (i) Own opinion **1 mark** for • a simple reason **2 marks** for • a developed reason • or two simple reasons **3 marks** for • three simple reasons • or two developed reasons • or a fully developed reason (ii) Why some people may disagree with their opinion **1 mark** for • a simple reason **2 marks** for • a developed reason • or two simple reasons **3 marks** for • three simple reasons • or two developed reasons • or a fully developed reason	6

APPENDIX 7

TARGET SETTING RESOURCES

Target setting after the end of section test

1. After the test, return students' marked scripts, plus the relevant parts of the mark scheme.

2. Give them the Target Setting Table and explain how it is used. They should go through their test paper and answer the questions on the sheet by comparing their marks and answers with the mark scheme (they will only have answers for one section).

3. Give the students Target Setting Sheet 1 and explain how to use the answers from the Target Setting Table to set themselves specific targets on Target Setting Sheet 1.

4. Explain that Target Setting Sheet 1 should be used and not filed away. Students could put it on their notice board or paste it onto their file.

   They should look at it regularly and make sure they are doing what it says.

5. They should now complete the relevant page of Target Setting Sheet 1A (this could be done for homework).

Target setting from the mock exam

1. Set students the Edexcel specimen assessment paper as their mock examination.

2. After the exam, return students' marked scripts, plus the published mark scheme.

3. Give them the Target Setting Table. Explain that they should use it in the same way as for the four sections, but this time filling in all four columns.

4. Give the students Target Setting Sheet 1. Explain how to use the answers from Target Setting Table to set themselves specific targets on Target Setting Sheet 1.

5. Explain that Target Setting Sheet 1 should be used and not filed away. Students could put it on their notice board or paste it into their file.

   They should look at it regularly and make sure they are doing what it says, especially when doing their final revision.

6. Make sure that students look at their target setting sheets just before the examination so that they try to avoid making the same mistakes in the real exam that they made in the mock exam and the end of section tests.

Target Setting Table

Questions	Section 1	Section 2	Section 3	Section 4
1. How many marks did I get for question a)?				
2. How many marks did I get for question b)? If less than 4:				
● Did I forget to give reasons?				
● Did I forget to develop my reasons?				
3. How many marks did I get for question c)? If less than 8:				
● Did I forget to use specialist vocabulary?				
● Did I describe instead of explain?				
● Did I misunderstand the question?				
● Did I give too few reasons or undeveloped reasons?				
● Did I forget about the Quality of Written Communication?				
4. How many marks did I get for question d)? If less than 6:				
● Did I forget to include one point of view from one religion?				
● Did I forget to use information from the specification?				
● Did I give too few reasons for part i)?				
● Did I give too few reasons for part ii)?				

Religion and Society Teacher's Resource Pack Third Edition © Hodder Education, 2009

TARGET SETTING SHEET 1

Using the Target Setting Table, circle the targets that apply to you.

1. Question a)

Marks	Target
2 marks	Make sure I still know all the key words.
1 or less marks	Learn the key words more thoroughly.

2. Question b)

Marks	Target
Yes to bullet point 1	Remember to give reasons for my opinion.
Yes to bullet point 2	Make sure I write developed reasons for my opinion.

3. Question c)

Marks	Target
Yes to bullet point 1	Remember to use the key words in my question c) answers. Learn and use specialist terms.
Yes to bullet point 2	Practise understanding questions so that I explain why or how.
Yes to bullet point 3	Ask the teacher to explain some past questions, then practise answering them.
Yes to bullet point 4	Make sure to give four reasons, or two developed reasons. If it is about different attitudes, make sure I give two reasons for why some agree and two reasons for why some disagree.
Yes to bullet point 5	Remember to take care with spelling and punctuation. Remember not to use bullet points.

4. Question d)

Marks	Target
Yes to bullet point 1	Make sure that either my own point of view or the ones that disagree with me is from a named religion.
Yes to bullet point 2	Make sure to use reasons from the lessons/text book/revision note or guide.
Yes to bullet point 3 or 4	Make sure to give three reasons for each part.

TARGET SETTING SHEET 1A

End of section 1

WHAT I HAVE LEARNT FROM SECTION 1

TEST RESULT FOR SECTION 1

NEXT TERM I WILL BE STUDYING

2.1 Global warming – its causes and possible solutions

2.2 Forms of pollution and their possible solutions

2.3 Issues connected with the scarcity of natural resources

2.4 Christian teachings on stewardship

2.5 The teachings of one religion other than Christianity on stewardship

2.6 The nature and importance of medical treatments for infertility

2.7 Different attitudes to infertility treatments among Christians

2.8 Attitudes to infertility treatments in one religion other than Christianity

2.9 The nature and importance of transplant surgery

2.10 Different attitudes to transplant surgery in Christianity

2.11 Different attitudes to transplant surgery in one religion other than Christianity

MY TARGETS FOR NEXT TERM ARE:

TARGET SETTING SHEET 1A

End of section 2

WHAT I HAVE LEARNT FROM SECTION 2

TEST RESULT FOR SECTION 2

NEXT TERM I WILL BE STUDYING

3.1   The United Nations and world peace, including one example of its work

3.2   How religious organisations try to promote world peace

3.3   Why wars occur, using examples from current conflicts

3.4   The nature and importance of the theory of just war

3.5   Differences among Christians in their attitudes to war

3.6   The attitudes to war of one religion other than Christianity

3.7   Christian attitudes to bullying

3.8   The attitudes to bullying in one religion other than Christianity

3.9   Religious conflicts within families

3.10 Christian teachings on forgiveness and reconciliation

3.11 The teachings on forgiveness and reconciliation of one religion other than Christianity

MY TARGETS FOR NEXT TERM ARE:

TARGET SETTING SHEET 1A

End of section 3

WHAT I HAVE LEARNT FROM SECTION 3

TEST RESULT FOR SECTION 3

NEXT TERM I WILL BE STUDYING

4.1   The need for law and justice

4.2   Theories of punishment and the arguments for and against them

4.3   Why justice is important for Christians

4.4   Why justice is important for the followers of one religion other than Christianity

4.5   The nature of capital punishment and non-religious arguments about capital punishment

4.6   Different attitudes to capital punishment among Christians

4.7   Different attitudes to capital punishment in one religion other than Christianity

4.8   The laws on drugs and alcohol and the reasons for them

4.9   Social and health problems caused by drugs and alcohol

4.10 Different attitudes to drugs and alcohol in Christianity and the reasons for them

4.11 Attitudes to drugs and alcohol in one religion other than Christianity

MY TARGETS FOR NEXT TERM ARE:

TARGET SETTING SHEET 1A

End of section 4

WHAT I HAVE LEARNT FROM SECTION 4

TEST RESULT FOR SECTION 4

NEXT TERM I WILL BE REVISING FOR THE FINAL EXAM

MY TARGETS FOR NEXT TERM ARE:

APPENDIX 8

LINKS TO THE CITIZENSHIP PROGRAMME OF STUDY

KS4 Citizenship Statutory	Coverage in Edexcel Religious Studies
Key concept 1 Democracy and justice	The whole of Units 1 and 8
Key concept 2 Rights and responsibilities	Unit 1, Sections 2 and 4 The whole of Unit 8
Key concept 3 identities and diversity	The whole of Units 1 and 8
All the key processes except 2.3c, d and e will be covered by the teaching and assessment methods of Units 1 and 8	Key processes 2,3c, d and e will be covered by resources in *Religion and Society Teacher's Resource Pack Third Edition*
3a – political, legal and human rights	Unit 8, Sections 1 and 4 Unit 1, Sections 2 and 4
3b – the role and operation of civil and criminal law and the justice system	Unit 8, Sections 1 and 4
3c – how laws are made by people and processes, including the work of parliament, the government and the courts	Unit 8, Sections 1 and 4
3d – actions citizens can take in democratic and electoral processes to influence decisions	Unit 8, Section 1 Unit 1, Sections 2 and 4
3e – the operation of parliamentary democracy within the UK and of other forms of government in the world	Unit 8, Sections 1 and 3
3f – the development of and struggle for different kinds of rights and freedoms in the UK	Unit 1, Sections 3 and 4 Unit 8, Sections 1 and 4
3g – how information is used in public debate and policy formation, including the media, pressure and interest groups	Unit 1, Sections 2, 3 and 4 Unit 8, Sections 1, 2 and 4
3h – the impact of individual and collective actions on communities	Unit 1, Sections 2, 3 and 4 Unit 8, Sections 1, 2, 3 and 4
3i – policies and practices of sustainable development and their impact on the environment	Unit 8, Section 2
3j – the economy in relation to citizenship	To be covered by resources in *Religion and Society Teacher's Resource Pack Third Edition*
3k – rights and responsibilities of consumers, employers and employees	To be covered by resources in *Religion and Society Teacher's Resource Pack Third Edition*
3l – the origins and implications of diversity and the changing nature of society in the UK	Unit 1, Section 4
3m – the UK's role in the world including the EU, Commonwealth and the UN	Unit 8, Section 3
3n – the challenges facing the global community	Unit 1, Section 2 Unit 8, Sections 2, 3 and 4
4 – curriculum opportunities a, b, c, f, g, h and i	Will be covered by most lessons in Units 1 and 8
4 – curriculum opportunities d, e and j	To be covered by resources in *Religion and Society Teacher's Resource Pack Third Edition*

APPENDIX 9: LINKS TO THE PSHE PROGRAMME OF STUDY

KS4 PSHE Non-Statutory	Coverage in Edexcel Religious Studies
Economic well-being	
a – different types of work, including employment, self-employment and voluntary work	Best covered in tutorial, but voluntary work would be developed in Unit 1, Section 4 and Unit 8, Sections 2 and 4
b – the organisation and structure of different types of businesses, and work roles and identities	Best covered in careers
c – rights and responsibilities at work and attitudes and values in relation to work and enterprise	To be covered in careers and by Appendix 10 in *Religion and Society Teacher's Resource Pack Third Edition*
d – the range of opportunities in learning and work and changing patterns of employment (local, national, European and global)	Tutorial/careers
e – the personal review and planning process	Tutorial
f – skills and qualities in relation to employers' needs	Tutorial
g – a range of economic and business terms, including the connections between markets, competition, price and profit	Appendix 10 in *Religion and Society Teacher's Resource Pack Third Edition*
h – personal budgeting, wages, taxes, money management, credit, debt and a range of financial products and services	Appendix 10 in *Religion and Society Teacher's Resource Pack Third Edition*
i – risk and reward, and how money can make money through savings, investment and trade	Appendix 10 in *Religion and Society Teacher's Resource Pack Third Edition*
Personal well-being	
a – the effects of diverse and conflicting values on individuals, families and communities and ways of responding to them	The whole of Units 1 and 8
b – how the media portrays young people, body image and health issues	Tutorial
c – the characteristics of emotional and mental health, and the causes, symptoms and treatments of some mental and emotional health disorders	Tutorial/science
d – the benefits and risks of health and lifestyle choices, including choices relating to sexual activity and substance use and misuse, and the short- and long-term consequences for the health and mental and emotional well-being of individuals, families and communities	Unit 1, Section 3 Unit 8, Section 4
e – where and how to obtain health information, how to recognise and follow healthy lifestyles	*Religion and Life Teacher's Resource Pack Third Edition*, Section 3 Tutorial/science
f – characteristics of positive relationships, and awareness of exploitation in relationships and of statutory and voluntary organisations that support relationships in crisis	Unit 1, Sections 3 and 4 Unit 8, Sections 3 and 4

KS4 PSHE Non-Statutory	Coverage in Edexcel Religious Studies
g – the roles and responsibilities of parents, carers, children and other family members	Unit 1, Section 3
h – parenting skills and qualities and their central importance to family life	Unit 1, Section 3
i – the impact of separation, divorce and bereavement on families and the need to adapt to changing circumstances	Unit 1, Sections 2 and 3
j – the diversity of ethnic and cultural groups, the power of prejudice, bullying, discrimination and racism, and the need to take the initiative in challenging this and other offensive behaviours and in giving support to victims of abuse	Unit 1, Section 4 Unit 8, Sections 3 and 4

APPENDIX 10

CITIZENSHIP RESOURCES

Citizenship Key Stage 4 Programme of Study areas 3b and 3c

Areas 3b and 3c of the Citizenship KS4 Programme of Study are concerned with student participation in school and community activities. Many students will be taking part in such activities without your being aware of it. At the beginning of Year 10, they should be given their Key Stage 4 activity record sheet to complete (if a similar sheet is already being used for their Record of Achievement, use this as their Key Stage 4 Citizenship record). Work experience is a Key Stage 4 Citizenship activity. These sheets should be kept by their tutor and be updated every term in tutor group. The Religious Studies teacher or tutor should try to get each student to complete a reflection sheet on one activity per year to keep with their activity record sheet. In Year 10 or 11, this should be their work experience record sheet.

If your school has a School Council, every student should complete the School Council record sheet each year and keep it in their Citizenship Portfolio (you will need to adapt this for those students who are council representatives).

To help those students who take part in few activities, you could try the following:

1. Any work that is being done for charity should include:
   - tutor group investigation, discussion and then voting on which charity to support
   - reflection on the event, including how more money could have been raised and how the organisation could have been improved.

2. If you do not have a School Council, your senior management should consider establishing one to ensure that all students take part in the school community. There is information on setting up a School Council on www.schoolcouncil.org.uk (or call 020 8349 2459). An invaluable resource for all school councils is *Secondary School Councils* (Di Clay, London, School Councils UK, 2001, ISBN 0953563928).

   Students should record their involvement in the School Council on the School Council record sheet.

3. Encourage inter-tutor group competition for Local Agenda 21 (LA 21). Clearing up litter, organising the recycling of cans, etc. is all a part of LA 21. If this is linked with their Citizenship investigation into LA 21, students should have ideas of what needs to be done. Alternatively, invite the local council in to assemblies to encourage student participation. This should be recorded on their Citizenship activity record sheet.

4. At Christmas, you could organise either toys for under-privileged children or food parcels for the elderly. Before organising anything like this, contact your local Social Services to ensure that there is a need and a means of delivering the gifts. If not, there may be opportunities to organise shopping, gardening, etc.

KEY STAGE 4 CITIZENSHIP ACTIVITIES RECORD SHEET

NAME .... TUTOR GROUP..............

School activity	Teacher in charge

Out-of-school activity	Organisation

WORK EXPERIENCE RECORD SHEET (PAGE 1)

NAME ....   TUTOR GROUP..............

1. How did I decide/negotiate my work experience placement?

2. What is the name of the firm, its address and telephone number and the name of my contact there?

3. What preparations should I make for work experience?

4. What happened on day 1?

WORK EXPERIENCE RECORD SHEET (PAGE 2)

5. What happened on day 2?

6. What happened on day 3?

7. What happened on day 4?

8. What happened on day 5?

WORK EXPERIENCE RECORD SHEET (PAGE 3)

9. What did I learn from my work experience?

10. Are there any things I would change in my choice/negotiations about work experience?

11. Are there any things I would change about my preparations for work experience?

12. Are there any things I would like to have changed about the way I behaved during work experience?

SCHOOL COUNCIL RECORD SHEET

NAME .... TUTOR GROUP............. YEAR 10, 11

Who is my group representative on the council?

How were they elected?

Action we asked our representative to take	Representative's report back from the council meeting	What happened?

My thoughts about the School Council this year:

REFLECTING ON CITIZENSHIP ACTIVITIES SHEET

What was the activity?

How and why did I decide to take part in this activity?

What have I learned from taking part in this activity?

What would I change if I were taking part in this activity again?

HOW THE ECONOMY FUNCTIONS, INCLUDING THE ROLE OF BUSINESS AND FINANCIAL SERVICES

Working in groups is an important part of covering this area of citizenship.

Before any of the activities provide students with the simple overview chart How The Economy Works (page 217) and make sure that they understand it. The objective is for students to have a basic understanding of where they and their family fit into the economy of the UK.

Activity 1

Working in groups of 4–6, ask the students to list their sources of income, for example, pocket money, part-time job, allowances, using Worksheet 1A.

In the same groups, ask them to list the ways in which they spend their money, for example, saving, donations, on themselves and others, using Worksheet 1B.

Using their income and spending Worksheets (1A and 1B) and the How The Economy Works chart, ask the groups to identify which of the items could be taxed.

Ask the groups to present their findings, and follow this with a discussion, amending answers where necessary.

Activity 2

Working in the same groups, ask the students to:
- list the sources of income for their household (parents' and carers' wages, interest on savings, etc.)
- list the ways the household income is spent (clothing, shelter, taxes, holidays, savings, pensions, insurance, etc.)
- identify which of the household income and spending items are taxed
- explain what happens when spending exceeds income (go through this point using the Financial Services chart provided on page 218).

Activity 3

(Use the How the Economy Works chart as an aide.)

Working in groups, ask students to discuss the following questions:
- How does the Government (local and national) get its income? For example, personal income tax, corporation tax, VAT, stamp duty. The students should identify which social group contributes which tax (individuals, manufacturers, financial services, etc.)
- Where does the Government spend the money it receives?
- Who benefits from Government spending?
- What happens when the Government needs more money?

Activity 4

Ask students to work in groups to create a flow chart from the work they have done that shows the student's place in the economy. They should list an individual's income and spending in greater detail than the How the Economy Works chart.

? ?

HOW THE ECONOMY WORKS

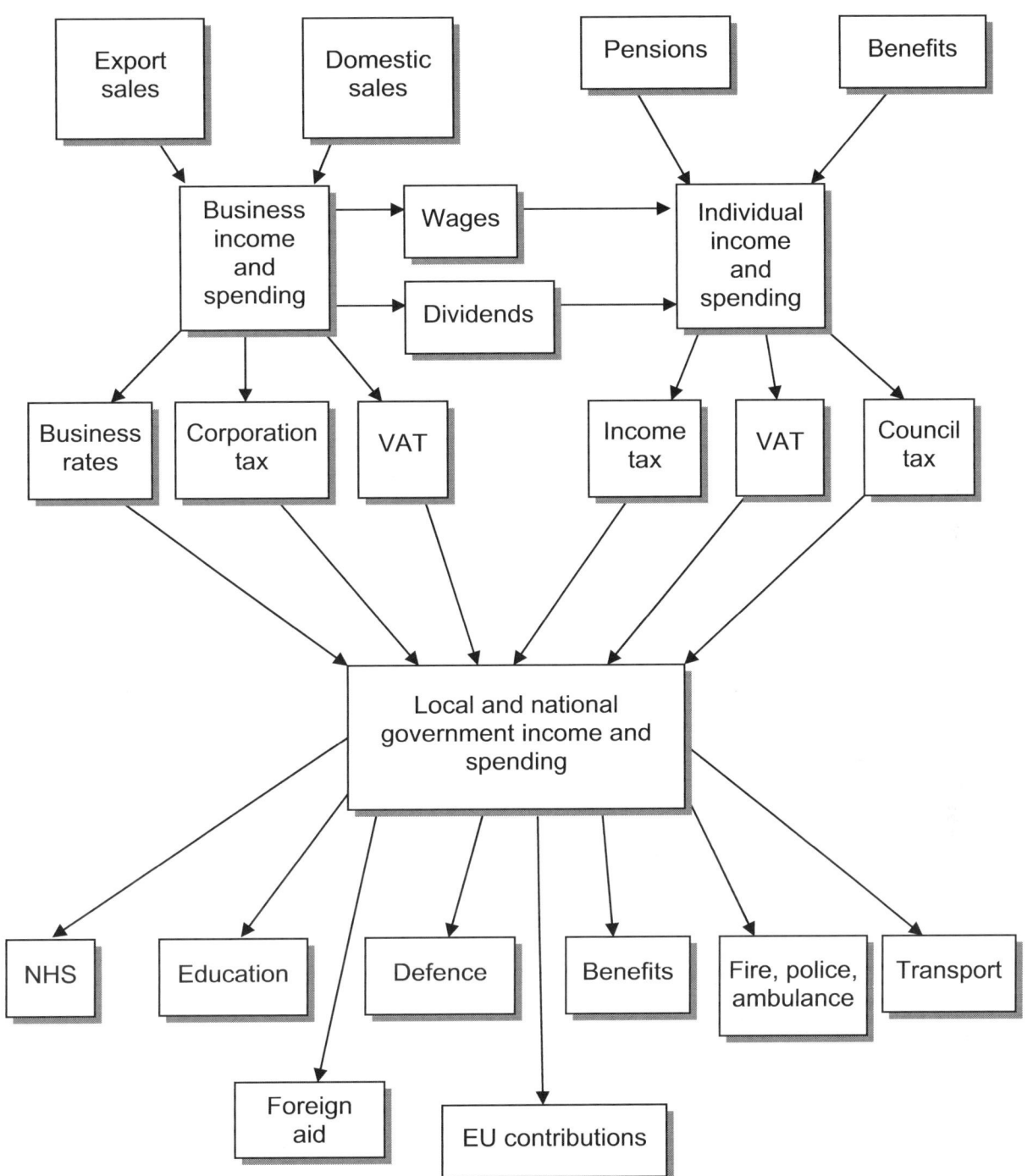

This is a very basic outline of how the economy works from a simplified viewpoint. It does not take into account:
- balance of payments
- government debt
- personal debt
- interest payments
- inheritance tax
- unearned income.

? ?

? ? ? ? ? ? ? ? ? ? ? ? ? ? ? ? ? ? ? ?

FINANCIAL SERVICES SECTOR BASIC CASH FLOW

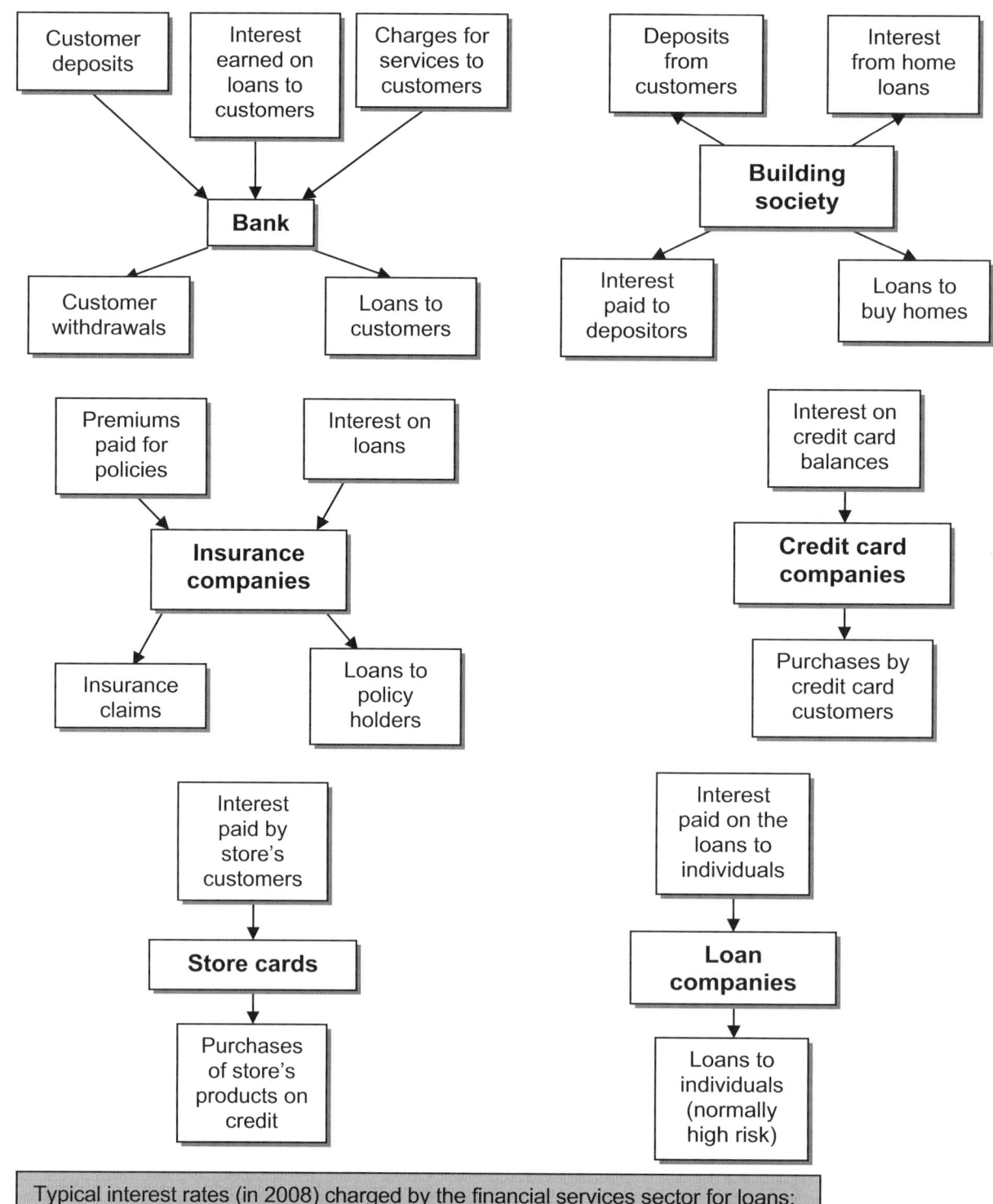

| Customer deposits | Interest earned on loans to customers | Charges for services to customers |

Bank

| Customer withdrawals | Loans to customers |

| Premiums paid for policies | Interest on loans |

Insurance companies

| Insurance claims | Loans to policy holders |

| Interest paid by store's customers |

Store cards

| Purchases of store's products on credit |

| Deposits from customers | Interest from home loans |

Building society

| Interest paid to depositors | Loans to buy homes |

| Interest on credit card balances |

Credit card companies

| Purchases by credit card customers |

| Interest paid on the loans to individuals |

Loan companies

| Loans to individuals (normally high risk) |

Typical interest rates (in 2008) charged by the financial services sector for loans:

Banks	7.8% to 8.9%
Building societies	5.7% to 6.3%
Credit card companies	15.9% to 17.9%
Store cards	29% +
Highest loan company	189.2%

? ? ? ? ? ? ? ? ? ? ? ? ? ? ? ? ? ? ? ?

WORKSHEET 1A

Sources of
my spending
money

WORKSHEET 1B

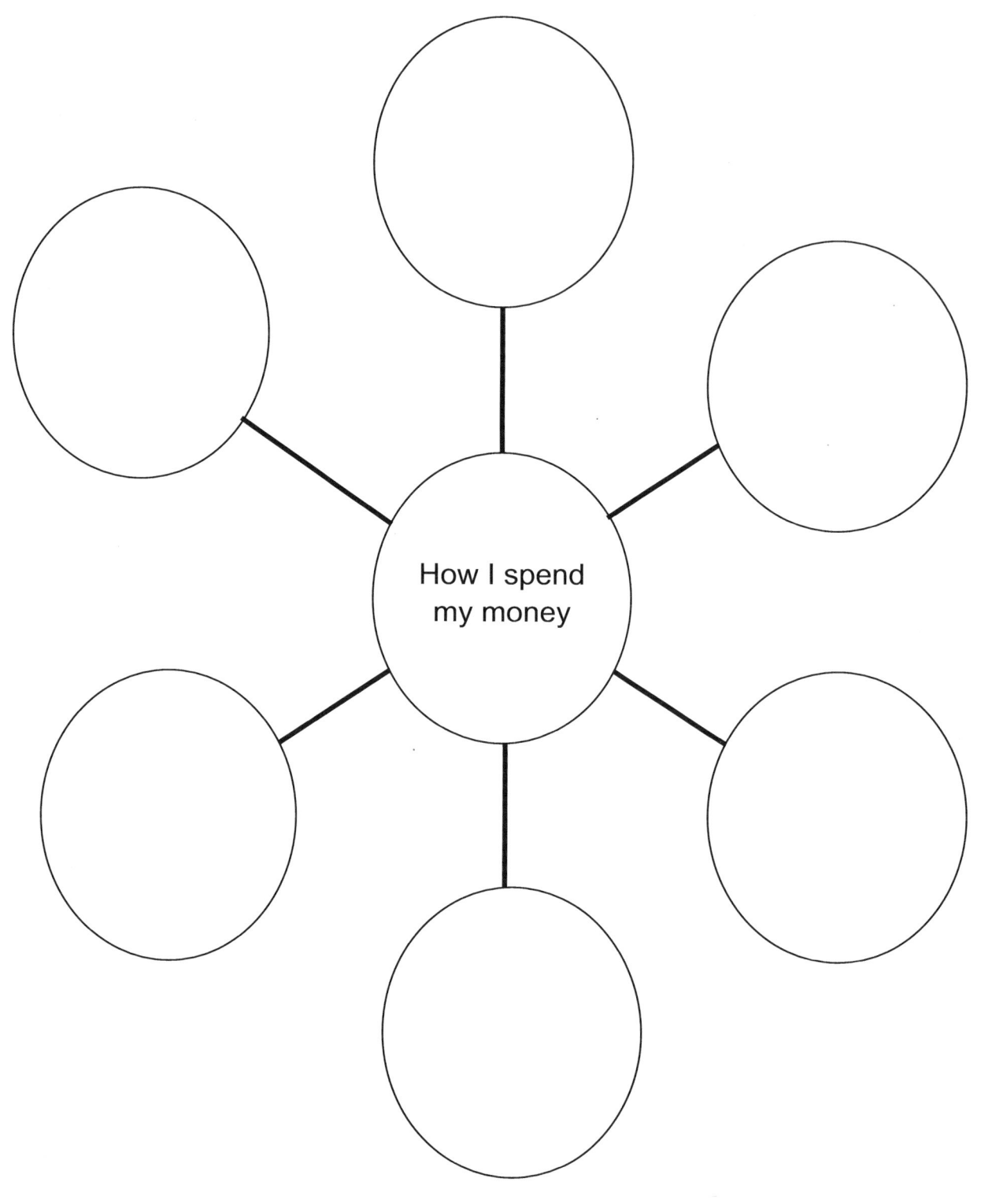

How I spend
my money